True Crime Stories

12 Shocking True Crime Murder Cases

True Crime Anthology Vol.3

By
Jack Rosewood

Copyright © 2016 by Wiq Media

ALL RIGHTS RESERVED

No part of this book may be reproduced, stored in a retrieval system, or transmitted in any form or by any means, electronic, mechanical, photocopying, recording, scanning, or otherwise, without the prior written permission of the publisher.

ISBN-13:978-1537283210

DISCLAIMER:

This crime anthology biography includes quotes from those closely involved in the twelve cases examined, and it is not the author's intention to defame or intentionally hurt anyone involved. The interpretation of the events leading up to these crimes are the author's as a result of researching the true crime murders. Any comments made about the psychopathic or sociopathic behavior of criminals involved in any of these cases are the sole opinion and responsibility of the person quoted.

Free Bonus!

Get two free books when you sign up to my VIP newsletter at www.jackrosewood.com
**150 interesting trivia about serial killers
and the story of serial killer Herbert Mullin.**

Contents

Introduction 1

CHAPTER 1: The Melaniee Road Murder Case 3

   A Good Girl 4

   A Vicious Attack 4

   The Case Goes Cold 6

   A Circuitous DNA Match 8

   The Trial and Unanswered Questions 10

CHAPTER 2: The Keddie Cabin Murders 12

   The Horror in Cabin 28 13

   The Sharp Family 14

   What is Known about the Crime 15

The Investigation 19

   A Rogues' Gallery of Suspects 22

   The Keddie Cabin Murders Today 28

CHAPTER 3: Joseph "The Axe Man" Ntshongwana 30

   The Axe Man 31

   From Rags to Riches 31

Stalking His Victims 32

A Bizarre Trial and New Revelations 34

CHAPTER 4: The Disappearance and Murder of Ryan Lane 37

The Disappearance 38

A Plan Gone Awry? 41

The Evidence 42

CHAPTER 5: The Torture and Murder of Junko Furuta 46

The Abduction 47

An Adult Crime but Juvenile Time 51

The Aftermath 53

CHAPTER 6: Christian Dornier's Rural French Massacre 56

Christian Dornier 58

The Massacre 61

Insanity Defense 64

CHAPTER 7: The Mysterious Murder of Jessica Lynn Keen 68

A Good Girl Gone Bad 68

Jessica's Murder 70

Modern Science Reveals the Killer 72

CHAPTER 8: Mattias Flink's Swedish Shooting Spree 75

Mattias Flink 77

Washing Falun in Blood 79

Life In and Out of Prison.. 81

CHAPTER 9: Matthew Tvrdon's White Van Rampage 85

The Death Van... 85

The Sentence... 89

CHAPTER 10: The Case of the Real Life Zombie, Tyree Smith 91

Eyeballs Taste Like Oysters 93

CHAPTER 11: The Cold Murder Case of Wilhelmina and Ed Maurin... 96

A Brutal Murder 97

Two Suspects Emerge 99

CHAPTER 12: The 1993 Long Island Railway Shooting Rampage.. 104

Colin Ferguson's Early Life 105

The Transition to a Race Warrior 108

Colin Ferguson's Race War.. 110

A Most Bizarre Trial... 111

The Aftermath of the Shooting 113

Conclusion... 115

Introduction

The world is a wonderful place, full of many amazing sights and people that bring joy to people's lives. We see the things that bring joy to people every day in a variety of different ways, from the smile of a child to the relaxing calm of nature. With that said, the world can also be an incredibly cruel and awful place that is full of heartless killers and deranged criminals. Because of the juxtaposition between joy and cruelty that the world presents, it is sometimes difficult for us to navigate around the darkness in order to enjoy the light.

Most people will never witness the cruel side of the world, but unfortunately those who do are often innocent and completely unaware of their situations.

Most of us have read or heard about the statistics that state the perpetrators of violence usually attack someone they know. We would like to think that we can defend against such attacks, or at least see them coming; but when a stranger attacks, it creates an entirely different dynamic for law enforcement and society.

Seemingly random acts of murder and mayhem leave the surviving victims and their families in pain and society wondering what would drive a person to commit such acts. Worse yet are the cases where a hapless victim is taken off the streets and murdered, only for the killer to escape justice.

In the following pages of this book, you will read about several crime cases from around the world where heinous crimes were committed by depraved souls, often at random. Most of these cases were eventually solved through diligent police work and a few lucky breaks.

But one of the most horrendous of these crimes, the Keddie cabin murders, still remains open.

Many of the crimes profiled in the pages of this book concern spree killers, often from countries with low crime rates. Oftentimes these killers used guns to claim their victims, like Christian Doriner, Mattias Flink, and Colin Ferguson; but others, such as Matthew Tvrdon, have proved that you do not need a gun to inflict multiple casualties.

So open the pages of this book, if you dare, and learn about some of the most bizarre crime cases from around the world in recent history.

CHAPTER 1:
The Melaniee Road Murder Case

Most people look back on their seventeenth year of life with fondness. Independence is right around the corner, but the protection of family and the law still allows one a level of comfort not known in adulthood. Many of us pushed and even broke the limits of family rules and the law at seventeen by experimenting with drugs, alcohol, and sex. But the majority of us come through that rebellious period a bit wiser and eventually move on to become productive members of society.

Of course there are those who never leave their adolescent rebellion behind and instead immerse themselves in various criminal activities.

Then there are those who never move past the rebellious attitude of age seventeen because they are murdered by people who continue to indulge their adolescent fantasies, no matter how old they are or how twisted the nature of their fantasies.

Melaniee Road was a seventeen-year-old whose flirtation with rebellion was randomly ended in murder one June night in 1984 by a sadistic killer. Melaniee's murder shocked and outraged her fellow British citizens who asked questions that could not be answered because there were few leads for the police to follow.

Eventually, due to advances in technology, Melaniee's murderer was eventually arrested and sent to prison, but the killer's capture only seemed to raise more questions in a case that was as bizarre as it was heart wrenching.

A Good Girl

In 1984, seventeen-year-old Melaniee Road was not the typical murder victim in the United Kingdom. She was a good student who was set to go to college, enjoyed spending time with her family, friends, and boyfriend, and was not involved in any criminal activity or drug use.

The attractive blonde also had no known enemies.

Because of her background, police were baffled as to who killed the young woman on the quiet streets of Bath on the morning of June 9, 1984.

A Vicious Attack

The night of June 8, 1984, began like many others for Melaniee Road. She met up with her boyfriend early in the evening and then the two walked to one of their favorite hangouts, the "Beau Nash" nightclub, where they met some friends.

After an evening of dancing and drinking, the group decided to call it a night at about 1:30 am, so they all said their goodbyes and went their separate ways. Melaniee had made the walk from her parent's home to the club and back numerous times without incident. In 1984, Bath had a low crime rate and there were no high crime areas she had to pass between the club and her house.

Unfortunately, she met a monster on her walk home.

Although there were no witnesses to the attack, police were able to piece together the sequence of events through physical evidence.

Melaniee's attacker mercilessly pounced on her on the sidewalk, stabbing her multiple times before she ran into a cul-de-sac. The cul-de-sac proved not only to be a dead end for the street, but also for Melaniee as the attacker then stabbed her several more times, twenty-six total. As the young woman lay bleeding to death on the lonely street, the killer could not contain his sadistic urges, so he raped her lifeless body.

Melaniee's body was discovered a few hours later in a pool of blood by a milkman who was making his daily deliveries with his ten-year-old son.

The local police immediately sealed the location and took biological evidence from the body, but DNA profiling was still unavailable to police departments in 1984.

With no biological evidence that they could immediately use, detectives turned to more traditional methods in order to capture Melaniee's killer. Attention was first focused on Melaniee's boyfriend, but it was quickly determined that he was not the killer as he had an air-tight alibi.

The police then received a tip that a young woman and a man were heard arguing loudly in the vicinity around the time of the murder. Investigators followed up the lead, but it proved to be another dead end.

Finally, with most of their resources exhausted and at their wit's end, the local police initiated "Operation Rhodium." The operation was essentially a dragnet in which ninety- four men who fit the profile of the killer were rounded up and arrested on various charges ranging from outstanding warrants to minor offences such as loitering. The operation proved to be a failure and worse yet the killer was one of the men arrested.

The killer had slipped right through their hands!

The Case Goes Cold

Unfortunately, due to scientific limits regarding DNA profiling and a lack of eye witnesses, the Melaniee Road murder case quickly went cold. It was not as if the young woman's family gave up; they continued to press the case in the media and with the local police. In the mid-1980s there was simply nothing the police could do, but the amount of biological evidence the killer left on Melaniee's body meant that eventually time was on the investigators' side.

Today, the process of DNA profiling has become so ubiquitous that few actually stop to consider the science or history behind it. Because we have become inundated with so many true crime documentaries and a plethora of crime procedural dramas, many think that DNA is something that is left behind at every crime scene and can be simply collected by investigators, leading to an arrest, all within a matter of hours.

Of course, the process is not so simple and it took a long time for it to become refined to the point where it is today.

Deoxyribonucleic acid (DNA), the building block of living organisms, was first identified by Swiss scientist Friedrich Miescher in 1869. The first several decades of DNA research focused on identifying and isolating inherited diseases, but the biggest advance, at least in terms of forensic police work, came in a lab in Leicester, United Kingdom. British scientist Alex Jefferys, from his Leicester lab just months after Melaniee's murder, discovered that each person has a unique DNA code that can be "fingerprinted."

Jefferys first used DNA profiling to help capture British murderer and rapist Colin Pitchfork in 1987, which set the stage for DNA profiling to be used in crime labs across the world.

Despite DNA profiling offering new hope to Melanie Road's family, the process had many problems in its first two decades of use. Samples too small or degraded, as was the case with Melanie Road, were often unable to be used and the process itself could take several months to create a complete profile. Databases that stored DNA profiles of criminal offenders also took several years to launch as time was needed for the computer technology to catch up with the advances made in DNA profiling.

By the early 2010s, the United Kingdom had amassed an extensive DNA database of criminal offenders so the authorities thought it was a good time to take another look at the Melanie Road murder case. The police began by taking DNA samples from hundreds of local Bath men, as well as rechecking the database for any hits.

But little did they know that the big break in the case would come from the DNA of a woman, not a man.

A Circuitous DNA Match

Clara Hampton never had the perfect life. She never seemed to end up in a good relationship and in 2014, at the age of forty-four, she found herself in another such situation with her, live-in boyfriend. The two became involved in a heated situation that turned physical, which resulted in the police showing up. Clara was booked on a minor charge that required her to give a mouth swab for the United Kingdom's DNA database.

The swab quickly put things in motion that solved the thirty-year murder mystery of Melanie Road.

Shortly after Clara's DNA was entered into the database, investigators working on the Road case were electrified to learn that they had a *partial* hit. DNA profiling had advanced quite a bit since 1987 so by 2014 scientists were able to match a sample with a *similar* profile. When investigators learned that the similar profile was from a woman, they knew that she did not commit the crime, but instead it was probably someone closely related to her, like a brother.

Or perhaps her father, Christopher John Hampton, who was originally brought in for questioning as a suspect during Operation Rhodium in 1984.

Hampton, who lived on the street where Melanie was murdered in 1984, was quickly picked up by police and given a DNA test. The findings were conclusive.

"Christopher Hampton's DNA was found to match the DNA from semen stains on the fly and crotch of Melaniee Road's trousers," said prosecutor Kate Brunner.

When the sixty-four-year old Hampton appeared in court, it was quickly revealed that he did not fit the typical psychological profile of such a killer. He was the father of four children and had been gainfully employed as a house painter throughout his life. Hampton also did not have a criminal record and was never linked to any criminal activity or drug use.

But it was all apparently just a façade, a mask, for a truly devious mind and soul that always lurked beneath.

The Trial and Unanswered Questions

Facing a mountain of physical and circumstantial evidence, Hampton decided to forgo a trial and instead pled guilty to murder in May 2016. When Hampton appeared in front of a judge for sentencing, he was a shell of his former self. He looked tired of life and gazed with no affect as the judge read the sentence.

Judge Andrew Popplewell looked straight at Hampton, sentenced the killer to a twenty two year minimum prison sentence, and said, "You will very likely die in prison." Because the United Kingdom does not have the death penalty and the crime rate is much lower there than in the United States, true "life sentences" are rarely given; but due to Hampton's age, as the judge said, the sadistic killer will likely die in prison.

After Hampton was sentenced, Melanie Road's friends and family said in interviews that they were glad the ordeal was finally over and that they were now able to find some closure, although the pain will never fully subside. They also indicated that were happy knowing that Hampton will never be able to victimize another young woman.

With that said, there are still some unanswered questions in the Melanie Road murder case.

"It hurts beyond repair," said Jean Road, mother of Melanie. "How can he do that to somebody and then live with people and with them not knowing?"

But somehow Christopher Hampton was able to keep his diabolical act a secret from those closest to him for over thirty years. Most people would never consider committing such a heinous crime and those who do often confess after several years out of guilt.

Apparently, Christopher Hampton has no conscience because one is required to feel a sense of guilt.

Hampton's lack of empathy and his apparent ability to keep his mouth shut leads one to wonder if he left more victims strewn about the United Kingdom. Presently, his DNA has not been linked to any other cold cases in the UK's database, but as the Melanie Road case proved, sometimes a strange coincidence and several years are needed to crack a cold case.

CHAPTER 2:
The Keddie Cabin Murders

Plumas County, California, is located in the northeast part of the state in the Sierra Nevada Mountains. The county is not very large in population, just over 20,000 inhabitants according to the 2010 census, but is quite large in size, which has resulted in a sparsely populated region where people have plenty of room to spread out.

The county was part of the gold rush in the middle of the nineteenth century, but has largely been bypassed in a number of ways in the 150 plus years since. There are no US highways or Interstates that run through the county and jobs have been as scarce as gold in more recent decades. Although the cost of living is quite low by California standards, the lack of employment and its isolation have combined to make Plumas County a place where few people move to who are looking for opportunities or to start over.

But starting over is exactly why Glenna Sue Sharp moved to Plumas County with her five children in 1980, except it turned out to be a fatal move and eventually ended up as one of the most bizarre cases in the annals of criminal history.

The Horror in Cabin 28

On the morning of April 12, 1981, the bodies of thirty-six-year old Glenna Sue Sharp, her fifteen-year-old son John Sharp, and his friend seventeen-year-old Dana Wingate were found beaten and stabbed to death in the living room of the Keddie, California, cabin that the mother shared with her children. The brutality of the crime shocked area residents and later the nation, as the victims appeared to have been killed randomly in a county that was known for having a low crime rate. As different media outlets quickly disseminated the details of the horrific attack, a new, appalling detailed was revealed.

Glenna's twelve-year-old daughter Tina was missing!

The Plumas County Sherriff's Department was quickly overwhelmed with the rapidly evolving situation—they had a triple murder *and* a missing person case on their hands. From the beginning, the investigation was bungled, which led to the Keddie cabin murders becoming a cold case that will probably never be solved.

Unfortunately, the victims of the Keddie cabin murders were in many ways the perfect victims: they were poor, had no powerful connections, and were not from the area.

The Sharp Family

When the perpetrator of a murder is not immediately known to detectives, their investigation usually begins with the victims. The police often begin their search of the victim, or in this case victims, backgrounds for signs of drug use or criminal activity. If neither of those are determined to be contributing factors in a person's murder, then investigators look at the victim's finances and/or if he/she may have been involved in a love triangle. In most cases, detectives are usually able to ascertain quickly that the victim was involved in one of these situations.

But in the case of the Keddie cabin murders, it was soon realized that a motive was not so clear.

A look the background of Glenna Sue Sharp, who usually went by her middle name, revealed that she was a divorced mother who was originally from Connecticut, but moved to northern California in 1980 to start over with her five children: John, Tina, ten-year-old Rick, five-year-old Greg, and fourteen-year-old Sheila. Plumas County investigators quickly ruled out a custody dispute gone bad because Sue's ex-husband was nowhere in the area when the crime happened and did not have the means to hire a killer. Also, the crime did not fit the typical custody dispute murder, as one of the children was killed and another was missing.

Sue did have money problems though.

The single mother found it difficult to find work that paid enough to support her five children, even though they lived in a relatively cheap cabin in an affordable county. Because of this, Sue was forced to rely on government assistance in order to make ends meet, but there was no evidence that she was in debt to loan sharks or any other criminal types.

Sue was described by her neighbors and acquaintances as a loner who spent most of her time with her children and let few people from outside of her familial circle get very close. She was known to date a few men in the area, but was not involved in a serious relationship at the time of her murder and none of her former suitors were known to harbor any acrimony towards her.

Sue was also not involved in any major drug activity and the police believed the other victims were simply too young to have created enemies who would go to such lengths for revenge.

The victims' backgrounds provided the Plumas County Sherriff's Department with few clues.

What is Known about the Crime

Despite finding dead ends with the victims' backgrounds, investigators found a mountain of physical evidence in the Sharp's cabin and were also lucky to have a possible eyewitness to the crime and numerous witnesses to the events that immediately led up to the horrific murders.

According to the accounts of surviving members of the Sharp family, as well as those from the Smartt family who lived next door in cabin 27, John Sharp and Dana Wingate were last seen walking down a road near the cabin on the evening of April 11. The two boys were hanging out that evening and planned to stay in John's basement bedroom, but were found the next morning dead in the upstairs living room.

The fact that the two boys were found dead in the living room with Sue Sharp was indeed mysterious to begin with, but it became even more so when investigators learned that John's bedroom did not have an entrance that led to the cabin. The only door in his downstairs bedroom led to the outside.

As the facts of the case came to light, it soon became obvious that the Keddie cabin murders were as enigmatic as they were brutal.

When Sheila Sharp returned home from a sleepover next door, she never imagined the horror that she would find. Almost immediately, the authorities suspected that more than one assailant was involved.

Murder in the real world is often a much more difficult affair than on television. It takes several minutes to kill someone from strangulation and beating and/or stabbing a person to death is usually quite loud and also takes some time. The killers are also often injured in stabbing and beating deaths. The fact that there were three victims suggests that either multiple assailants subdued the victims in a concerted attack, or a lone assailant used a gun to pacify the victims and then had one of his victims help bind the other two.

The victims were all bound with medical tape and electrical wires. The ligatures used on Sue were actually quite complex and suggest that she may have been the primary target and the other two were "collateral damage." The complex ligatures also suggest that the killer practiced ahead of time, had made ligatures before, or was possibly involved in a trade where knot tying was important.

Both Sue and John were stabbed several times and had their throats slit. Sue was also bludgeoned by what was later determined to be a pellet gun, although it was never recovered.

Some believe that Dana was forced to help the attacker(s) bind the other two and then he was killed last. The method of his murder was slightly different. He was strangled and then beaten with a hammer that was recovered several years later. Sue, John, and Dana suffered truly brutal deaths, which suggests that a personal vendetta was aimed at one of them. Since both of the boys were young and not known to be involved in criminal activity, the police believed that the primary target was Sue, but as will be discussed more below, determining a motive for her murder has been elusive.

A crime of truly horrific proportions took place in the Sharp family cabin on the night of April 11 or the early morning of April

12, which left the local authorities initially both baffled and alarmed, but the search for clues only seemed to turn up more questions instead of answers.

The sleepover that Shelia returned from was in cabin 27, which was located next door only about fifteen feet away. Neither she nor anyone in the cabin heard anything on the night of the eleventh or the morning of the twelfth. One would think that the brutal murders of three people would have created some significant sounds—a victim screaming, thuds of the bodies, or perhaps the killer(s) leaving the scene of the crime.

Even more amazing was the fact that three children were asleep in the room *next* to where the murders took place.

When the Plumas County Sherriff's Department cleared the crime scene, they soon discovered that Greg and Rick Sharp, along with neighbor boy, twelve-year-old Justin Smartt, were in a bedroom that was located on the other side of a wall from where the murders took place. Deputies pulled the three boys from one of the bedroom windows, but they were stunned to learn that none of them heard any commotion during the night. They apparently slept through the entire event!

Once the authorities learned what had happened, they were then faced with another problem—Tina was missing. In the weeks, months, and years following the Keddie cabin murders, the local authorities were criticized for not doing more to find Tina and taking too long to begin the search. Once the search began, efforts were made to find the girl with 1981 technology. Helicopters, dogs, horseback search teams, and distribution of Tina's picture on flyers around the area were all employed to find the girl, but they were all to no avail.

In 1984, in neighboring Butte County about thirty miles from Keddie, remains of an adolescent female skull were discovered in a rural area. The remains were later determined to be those of Tina Sharp—the number of Keddie cabin murder victims went to four.

The Investigation

From the beginning, the investigation of the Keddie cabin murders was flawed. It is true that the Plumas County Sherriff's Department did not have, and still does not have, the resources or seasoned investigators that larger police departments possess, but their investigators made a number of major mistakes throughout the investigation pertaining to witness interviews, crime scene investigation, evidence storage, and the search for Tina. Those who have followed the case over the last thirty-five years point to the mistakes of the Plumas County Sherriff's Department as the primary reason why the case has never been solved.

One of the biggest problems in the investigation was the eyewitness account of Justin Smartt. During his interview with investigators, Smartt at first claimed to have seen two white males leave cabin 28 sometime during the night. Sketch artists were brought in and composites were created of the two possible suspects, but Smartt's story began to change. In subsequent interviews, Smartt claimed that he thought what he saw that night was actually part of a dream. The boy's confusion was natural considering the traumatic event he lived through, which could have been remedied with other interrogation methods such as hypnotism.

But investigators apparently lost interest in Smartt and turned their energies elsewhere.

Another mistake that is often pointed to by critics of the police who have investigated the Keddie cabin murders in more recent years is the lack of proper crime scene management by the Plumas County Sherriff's Department. Investigators and even civilians were allowed to walk through the scene, perhaps destroying valuable forensic evidence in the process.

In fairness to the Plumas County Sherriff's Department, 1981 was several years before DNA profiling was a reality and almost fifteen years before the CODIS system was operational in the United States. With that said, police departments in 1981 knew that not only was proper management of a crime scene vital to a criminal investigation, but that the correct collection and storage of biological and forensic evidence was essential to solving a case.

Although DNA profiling was not known yet, blood typing did exist in 1981, and of course fingerprint identification had been used for about 100 years at that point. If the biological and forensic evidence in the Keddie cabin murders had been stored in the Plumas County crime lab properly, they may have led to the perpetrator(s) being caught at a later time.

Unfortunately, all of the forensic evidence connected to the Keddie cabin murders has been either lost or destroyed. When asked about the situation, the Plumas County Sherriff's Department refused to comment to the media on the missing evidence and in fact have been seen as somewhat hostile towards the media on this topic. The Plumas County Sherriff's Department also, for the most part, refused the help of state and federal agencies in the Keddie cabin murders. The overall attitude of the Plumas County Sherriff's Department towards the media and outsiders has been viewed as mysterious and suspicious by many and has raised several questions.

Why would the Plumas County Sherriff's Department, which was understaffed and ill-equipped to handle such a high profile case, not welcome the help of California state and federal law enforcement agencies? Does the Plumas County Sherriff's Department have something to hide, or is it just an agency full of stubborn individuals?

Concerned citizens have pressed for answers to these questions for decades.

A Rogues' Gallery of Suspects

Although the Plumas County Sherriff's Department dropped the ball on numerous occasions during the Keddie cabin murders investigation, their investigators quickly turned up a number of potential suspects and persons of interest.

As already mentioned above, Plumas County is a picturesque part of California with a relatively low crime rate—today and in 1981. Most people know their neighbors and it is still, even after the grisly murders, a place where many people keep their doors unlocked.

But underneath the quaint façade of 1981 Plumas County was a seedy underbelly teaming with a rogues' gallery of characters.

The investigation quickly revealed that Plumas County was home to an ample number of drug dealers, biker gang members, sex-offenders, ex-convicts, and various other local toughs. Truly, Plumas County in 1981 in many ways looked less like a Norman Rockwell painting than it did a setting in a rural crime drama such as *Justified* or *Banshee*.

First, there was Tina's teacher who was said to have an unhealthy interest in the girl. The teacher was a suspect and was later convicted of a sex crime, making him a registered sex offender in the state of California.

Then there was Robert Silveria Junior. Silveria, also known as the "Boxcar Killer," was a train hoping hobo who was associated with the violent hobo gang, Freight Train Riders of America (FTRA). Silveria earned quite a reputation among his fellow FTRA members by killing at least nine people throughout the western United States. Silveria was known to be in Plumas County in 1981 and claimed one of his victims not far from the Keddie cabin murder scene.

A couple of local toughs, Dee Jay Lake and Tony Garedakis, were also considered suspects by law enforcement and still are to some who continue to follow the case.

Sue's former boyfriends were also looked at along with other sex offenders and drug dealers who lived within a stone's throw of cabin 28. Despite the plethora of viable suspects, investigators soon began to focus on a pair who lived right next to the Sharp family.

Martin Ray Smartt was the father of Justin Smartt and the husband of Sue Sharp's friend, Marilyn. The Smartt family lived in cabin 26 with one of Martin's friends, a Chicago native named Bo Boubede. The Smartt and Sharp families were by all appearances good neighbors. The children all got along and played with each other, and the adults were also friendly and would occasionally go out together.

But a number of circumstances quickly made Martin and his friend Bo prime suspects in the Keddie cabin murders.

Some of Justin's recollections of the night of April 11 seemed to implicate his father and when investigators questioned Martin, they were left with even more questions.

According to Martin's statements to the Plumas County Sherriff's Department, he, his wife, and Bo Boubede had stopped by the Sharp home on the night of April 11 to ask Sue to join them for some drinks at a local bar. Sue declined and they left, which ended up being the last time anyone saw Glenna Sue Sharp alive. Martin claimed that the three then went to the bar and later returned home.

The story sounded believable to investigators, but it soon became a problem when Marilyn and Bo's stories diverged from Martin's.

Marilyn corroborated most of her husband's story, but added some very interesting details that helped investigators learn more about Martin's personality and his state of mind on the night of the murders. She claimed that the three did indeed go to the bar that night, but Martin became enraged at the volume and type of music being played at the bar. After having a few drinks, Martin led the three back to his home where he then called the bar and shouted some profanities to the bartender about the music. Marilyn then added that Martin was an abusive man who would turn to violence if he did not get things his way, especially with women.

Although Martin Smartt began to look like a more viable suspect, the Plumas County Sherriff's Department was unable to get a truly damning statement from him, but the Justice Department began to take an interest in the case.

In the United States, the crime of murder, no matter how heinous, is almost always covered under state law. Sometimes the FBI will get involved in murder investigations if the suspected killer has traveled across state lines or is believed to be part of some type of terrorist cell, but most murders are usually investigated by local, county, and/or state police. In the case of the Keddie cabin murders, there was also a kidnapping, which falls under the purview of the FBI.

The Justice Department's investigation of the Keddie cabin murders can be described as uninspired and routine at best. Martin Smartt was brought in to their offices in Sacramento for a polygraph exam, which he passed. The focus of the investigation then shifted from Martin to his friend Bo, but in recent years information has been made public that implicates the former in the murders.

Martin Smartt died in 1990, taking to the grave the answers to the Keddie cabin murders, many believe. In 2000, Smartt's former therapist came forward to the media and claimed that Smartt admitted his role in the murders. According to the therapist, Smartt killed Sue Sharp out of anger because she was apparently trying to convince his wife to leave him due to his physical and mental abuse. The two boys were "collateral damage" and Justin Smartt did in fact see his dad leave the cabin that night.

The "confession" sure sounds like solid evidence, but the reality is that even if Smartt were still alive, there is a good chance that it may not be admissible in court, as it was a violation of the doctor-patient privileged relationship. The credibility of the therapist would also be questioned: why come forward at that time and not earlier?

As investigators focused most of their attention on Martin Smartt as their primary suspect, his friend John "Bo" Boubede looked like he may be good as the second man seen outside cabin 28 on the night of April 11, 1981.

As stated above, Bo Boubede was with Martin and Marilyn Smartt on the night of the murders, drinking heavily at the local bar and the Smartt home. When questioned by investigators, Boubede gave numerous conflicting and strange stories that only helped to cast more suspicion on him. For instance, he gave different times concerning when he and the Smartts were at the bar in order to fit an alibi and for some reason he told police that he was impotent. Boubede would have had no reason to tell the police about his erectile dysfunction unless he was attempting to alibi himself for the rape or attempted rape of Sue.

Boubede also told investigators that he was a former police officer.

Even with limited 1981 technology, it did not take investigators long to learn that Boubede was the furthest thing from a cop. He had a record of violence and was a known associate of notorious Chicago hitman Jim Rini.

Boubede, like Smartt, was called into Sacramento to take a polygraph exam and also like his friend he passed. Later, sources revealed that both exams were extremely easy and full of leading questions.

If Boubede was involved in the Keddie cabin murders, he escaped justice in this world when he died in 1988.

Perhaps one of the most interesting and bizarre twists to the Keddie cabin case came a few months after Tina Sharp's skull was discovered. An anonymous call came into the Butte County Sherriff's Department that claimed the recently discovered human skull was that of Tina Sharp. Because DNA profiling did not exist yet in 1984, the phone call proved to be the key to identifying the skull and therefore determining what happened to the missing girl. The call was taped and a backup was made. The police believed that the call would be the break they needed to solve the case.

But for some reason, a law enforcement officer, whose identity remains unknown to the present day, lost both the original and backup tape.

It seems as though someone, or something, wants the Keddie cabin murders to remain a mystery.

The Keddie Cabin Murders Today

As the years went by, the residents of Keddie and Plumas County eventually went back to life as normal. The memories of the horrendous crimes began to recede in the minds of most people and the police investigation seemed to permanently stall. In the era before the Internet, the case still became an urban legend and cabins 27 and 28 became a sort of pilgrimage site for amateur ghost hunters, gawkers, and kids out for some cheap thrills.

Cabins 27 and 28 were demolished in 2004, erasing forever any physical reminders of the horrors that took place there in 1981.

But not everyone has forgotten about the Keddie cabin murders.

A new generation of tech savvy individuals became intrigued with the case, for reasons beyond simple curiosity or macabre fascination like the gawkers mentioned above. The recent generation of interest in the Keddie Cabin murders has seen some talented filmmakers and investigators who have taken it upon themselves to get to the bottom of this bizarre mystery.

Documentarian Josh Hancock wrote a book and produced an accompanying film in 2008 titled, *Cabin 28: The Keddie Murders*. Hancock explores several of the mysterious issues of the case described above in this book and offers his own take on who he believes committed the murders.

There is also a website—keddie28.com—that serves as the clearing house of the ongoing investigation and allows those interested to give their own opinions on the message board.

The Keddie cabin murders may unfortunately never be solved, but if they are it will be because ordinary, everyday citizens with an interest in the case, like Josh Hancock, will uncover definitive proof that reveals the killer or killers.

CHAPTER 3:
Joseph "The Axe Man" Ntshongwana

Most of you reading this are familiar with the case of the "Blade Runner" Oscar Pistorius. For those of you who are not familiar with the case, Pistorius is a South African runner who competed in the 2012 summer Olympics despite being a double amputee. He ran on artificial limbs, which is how he acquired the moniker the Blade Runner because the carbon-fiber prosthetics he uses to run are curved like blades. Pistorius captured the imagination and hearts of people across the world who saw him as a role model for people with disabilities.

But all of that changed when he shot his model girlfriend to death in 2013. In an instant, Pistorius went from national hero to absolute zero.

Pistorius is currently serving a six year prison sentence in a South African prison for the killing and there is no doubt that the charmed life he once knew as a sports star and national hero is now over.

But before the precipitous rise and fall of the Blade Runner, South Africans witnessed another one of their most popular sports stars take a violent fall from his pedestal.

The Axe Man

In 2011, South Africans were surprised to learn that former rugby union star Phindile Joseph Ntshongwana had been charged with the murders of four men. As residents read the details of the crime, their shock turned to horror when they discovered that Ntshongwana hacked to death and decapitated his victims with an axe.

What could make a man who had it all do such a thing?

From Rags to Riches

Ntshongwana was born in the mid-1970s during the height of the Apartheid regime in South Africa. He grew up in a poor segregated neighborhood where one of his primary outlets was sports, but even that was influenced by the social standards of the time. Blacks preferred to play soccer while whites gravitated towards rugby and cricket, but because of his stocky build, Ntshongwana chose rugby as his favorite sport.

Ntshongwana played rugby in segregated leagues for most of his childhood, which only offered advancement to a minimal level for the gifted player. Things changed, though, for Ntshongwana and South Africa when apartheid ended in 1994, giving the young man the chance to play in South Africa's top leagues, thereby earning the type of money and fame that few blacks, or even whites for that matter, could ever dream of.

By the late 1990s Ntshongwana was on his way!

The height of Ntshongwana's career came in 2010 when his team the Blue Bulls won the title of South Africa's top rugby league. The notoriety thrust the thirty-five-year-old Ntshongwana to the heights of fame and fortune and made him one of the most recognizable and popular figures in South Africa, with both blacks and whites.

But just a year later the life that took decades for Ntshongwana to build came crashing down in a matter of days.

Stalking His Victims

According to Ntshongwana, his charmed life was shattered in March 2011 when he learned that his daughter had been gang-raped and infected with HIV. The rugby player believed that the corrupt and incompetent police in South Africa would not be able to find the rapists, even if they bothered to look, so he decided to take the law into his own hands.

Ntshongwana grabbed a Bible and an axe and drove from his affluent neighborhood to the poverty and crime-stricken townships of Durban in order to find his prey. Witnesses to the crimes and Ntshongwana himself related to authorities the sequence of events, which were as brutal as they were bizarre.

On March 20, 2011, Ntshongwana read scriptures from the Bible and slinked around the township looking for his victims. He took the life of one of his victims that day, the second on the following, the third on day three, and the fourth victim a week later. The fact that a high-profile professional athlete went on a two week killing spree while reading the Bible is bizarre enough—the number of victims and one week "cooling off" period actually places him in the serial killer category—but the details of what he did to his victims truly place this case in the realm of the outlandish.

Court testimonies state that before killing some of his victims, Ntshongwana stripped naked, rubbed yogurt over his body, and then made his victims lick it off. One can only guess why he did this: probably to emasculate and degrade his victims before killing them, but it is impossible to say for sure. After hacking his victims to death, he then decapitated the bodies, placing the various body parts in garbage cans throughout Durban. Many of his victims' body parts were never found, but a head was discovered in a garbage can one mile from one of Ntshongwana's murder scenes.

When the details of Ntshongwana's crimes were made public, many were horrified, yet others took a more neutral attitude towards the case. Since the end of apartheid, crime has skyrocketed in the African nation, with carjackings, home invasions, and gang-rapes becoming fairly common crimes. In fact, many HIV-infected men from the most backward regions of the country believe that raping a virgin will cure them of the incurable disease. Because of these stark realities, many South Africans have grown numb to even the most brutal reports of crime in their country.

But Joseph Ntshongwana was different; he was after all a wealthy celebrity.

Those who did follow the case soon began to make comparisons with the O.J. Simpson trial in the United States. To some, it was the case of an entitled athlete who thought he was above the law, while to others it was situation where a man was wrongly accused, or perhaps overcharged.

Both sides were able to follow the heavily publicized trial when it took place in the years following the murders.

A Bizarre Trial and New Revelations

After Ntshongwana was arrested, Durban police investigated the accusation that he killed the men in retaliation for raping his daughter. The police announced that they could find no evidence that the former rugby player's daughter was raped.

It seems that Ntshongwana made up a story that would be believable in a country where such crimes are fairly common.

But if the men did not rape his daughter, why did he kill them?

The answer to this question, which is perhaps the first that anyone who knows about the case asks, will probably never be answered if the strange behavior that Ntshongwana exhibited during his trial is any indication of his state of mind.

When Ntshongwana was brought before a judge during his arraignment, he clutched a Bible and spoke in gibberish, or what some have described as "tongues." He interrupted the judge on numerous occasions and shoved the bailiffs when they tried to intercede. To all in observance, Ntshongwana truly looked like a deranged man.

Not long after the fiasco of his arraignment, Ntshongwana's father claimed he suffered from bi-polar disorder.

The groundwork was laid for an insanity defense.

Despite his bizarre behavior in and out of the court room, a judge ruled that Ntshongwana was competent to stand trial in February 2012. Paul Ntshongwana was convicted of five counts of murder in 2014 and sentenced to life in prison without parole.

After the conviction, the South African media quit featuring stories about the crimes of Joseph Ntshongwana so many entirely forgot about the sport star's fall from grace. Although Ntshongwana may have dropped from the thoughts of most people, South African police have kept an open file on the former rugby star. Since his incarceration, Ntshongwana has been accused of kidnaping and raping a woman in a 2010 incident.

Will more notorious crimes be linked in the future to South Africa's Axe Man? Only time and possibly forensic evidence will be able answer that question.

CHAPTER 4:
The Disappearance and Murder of Ryan Lane

The modern world has provided all of us with some pretty amazing things that have made our lives easier. Cars and airplanes have made travel a breeze, while dishwashers, washers, and dryers have allowed us to have easier domestic lives.

And who can live without a smart-phone?

It is true that science and technology have made life in industrialized countries easier in some ways, but psychologists, psychiatrists, and sociologists have argued that our use of, and some would say dependence on, technology in our daily lives has been a major factor in the decline of interpersonal relationships.

One does not have to look very far to see some signs of this trend. Couples at restaurants out for dinner spend more time on their phones then they do talking with each other and people everywhere live in a virtual world where updating their social media sites is more important than developing relationships in the real world.

Marriage has long been considered one of the casualties of the modern age and now that we are firmly in the age of Internet, divorce rates are steadily increasing in the most industrialized nations.

Despite the now ubiquitous nature of divorce in the modern world, most people who find themselves in one eventually move on with their lives. Of course, things are more difficult when children are involved. Custody disputes can quickly turn an amicable divorce into one full of acrimony. Allegations of misconduct can be made and sometimes more than just feelings are hurt. Even so, most custody disputes end peaceably as both parents realize that years of bickering will only serve to further alienate their children and that a child needs to have a good relationship with both parents.

But in some rare cases, one of the parents involved in a custody dispute believes that he or she and the children involved will be better served if the other parent is taken out of the equation.

The Disappearance

In February 2012, Ryan Lane was a twenty-four-year old father living in Calgary, Alberta, who was hoping to get closer to his young daughter. Life had not been particularly easy for Lane. He had trouble finding decent-paying employment and did not get along very well with the mother of his daughter, an ex-girlfriend who had fulltime custody of their child.

Despite these setbacks, Lane was young and determined to put his life on a positive path. He was working and had recently spoken with a lawyer about establishing specific times to see his daughter. His daughter's mother, Sheena Cuthill, was protective of the child to the point of obsession and would rarely let Lane visit her. Initially, Lane was fine with the arrangement, but once he matured a little he decided he wanted to develop a relationship with his child.

Lane won a judgement in family court that allowed him visitation of his daughter. On February 6, 2012, he met with Cuthill at a local pizza restaurant to discuss the details of the visitation agreement.

All seemed well for Lane.

Then the next day Lane received a mysterious call from a stranger who asked to meet with him to discuss a custody arrangement. Lane's family was immediately disturbed by the call and Ryan's father Bruce warned against him going to the meeting.

"What's he gonna do, stab me, or something?" said Ryan to Bruce.

Bruce pleaded with his son to let him come along, but Ryan insisted he go alone, as that was what the caller had stated. Ryan then walked to a nearby strip mall to meet the mysterious caller, but his father followed behind in his car despite his son's objections.

Bruce Lane then watched as his son got into a red pickup, which then drove off.

Ryan Lane was never seen again!

As hours turned to days, it was clear to Ryan Lane's family that something bad had happened to him. A missing person report was filed with the Calgary Police Department, and detectives followed up on the information about the custody dispute, the mysterious caller and the red truck. Although the situation looked suspicious to investigators and the Lane family was sure something had happened to Ryan, the Calgary police had no solid evidence that foul play was involved.

As the cold Calgary winter turned to spring and then summer, news reports of Ryan's disappearance faded and it seemed to some that police interest in the case had also waned.

But the reality was that detectives were looking closely at Sheena Cuthill and her associates due to some tips they had received and a growing amount of physical and circumstantial evidence they had collected.

But there was still no body.

Murderers are sometimes convicted without the body of the victim ever being discovered, but prosecutors will tell you that their job is much easier if they have a body. Juries often tend to be skeptical and require plenty of evidence to convict a person of murder, especially in today's world where both documentary and fictional television shows that profile the use of forensic evidence to solve crimes are commonplace.

In November 2012, the search for Ryan Lane finally came to an end when the charred remains of a human were discovered in a burn barrel in a remote area of northeast Calgary known as Beiseker. Although investigators believed they had found Ryan's final resting place, the degraded nature of the body could not be identified through DNA profiling. A forensic anthropologist was able to determine that the remains were of a person between the ages of nineteen and thirty, which fit Lane's age; but most importantly, a ring that Ryan's family identified as belonging to him was found in the pile of ashes.

It seems the killer or killers had made their first mistake.

The location of Ryan's remains would later prove to be a key piece of circumstantial evidence.

A Plan Gone Awry?

Once Ryan's remains were discovered, homicide investigators were able to piece together the other evidence they had been collecting in the prior months to produce an arrest warrant for Sheen Cuthill, her husband Timothy Rempel, and his brother Wilhelm "Will" Rempel for the murder of Ryan Lane. Based on statements the defendants gave to police and Cuthill's testimony at her murder trial, it was learned that the three plotted against Lane in order to prevent him from seeing his daughter.

According to Cuthill, the initial plan was just to intimidate and scare Lane away, but things quickly got out of hand. She claimed that the three met on the morning of February 6, 2012, at Cuthill's grandmother's home in northeast Calgary to discuss the details of the plan.

"I was expecting there was going to be a little rough-housing. I assumed there was going to be some fighting," stated Cuthill in a Calgary courtroom. "I didn't think what they were going to do to make it succeed."

Cuthill's courtroom testimony was valuable in answering who Ryan Lane met on February 7—Tim and Will Rempel—but it was short on important details. Essentially, Cuthill attempted to shift culpability in the murder from herself to the Rempel brothers.

But the mountain of evidence against all three clearly demonstrated that each was equally responsible for Ryan's death.

The Evidence

When Sheena Cuthill and the Rempel brothers went to trial, they faced an uphill battle trying to refute what seemed like an endless line of evidence against them. Although much of the evidence was circumstantial, there was just so much of it that it could not possibly be explained away and the few bits of forensic evidence the prosecutors did have only served to corroborate the circumstantial evidence.

One of the most damning pieces of physical evidence in the case was the discovery of Ryan Lane's DNA in both Will Rempel's truck, which happened to be red like the one Ryan was seen getting into, and Tim Rempel's jeep. The presence of the DNA could be explained away by a good defense lawyer perhaps, but it did not look good for the two brothers when it was revealed that they were caught on camera cleaning both vehicles inside and out the day of Ryan's disappearance. It was also extremely suspicious that Will sold his truck, which was in good condition, to a salvage yard the next day for the far under blue book value price of just $128.40!

The location where Ryan's remains were discovered also happened to become strong circumstantial evidence used against the Rempel brothers.

The burn barrel was located not far from a neighborhood where the brothers had both lived. Even more incriminating was the fact that both men had also worked at one time at the barrel's exact location!

Perhaps the evidence that contributed most to the legal demise of the three defendants were the details of the crime they sent each other via text messages. Maybe they thought they would never be suspects in any crime if Ryan's body was never found, or possibly they did not think their messages were saved, but the text messages were most damning because they essentially outlined the anatomy and chronology of the murder.

A 2011 series of texts between Cuthill and her husband, just after the courts awarded visitation rights to Lane, clearly implicate the mother in the conspiracy.

"Can I trust Will to have this done without the cops showing up on my doorstep?" Cuthill asked Tim Rempel.

In another message, Cuthill tried to allay Tim Rempel's fears of getting caught.

"You won't have any part in his mister ur gonna behanve n let ur brother deal with it," she texted like a teenager. "I mean it Tim my answer will be no right now I won't even consider it if you have any part of it."

Within a couple of months Tim Rempel's trepidation passed as a text he sent to his wife just two days before Ryan's abduction demonstrates.

"Getting things ready scoured the best spot at the pit."

To add to the incriminating text messages, the police secretly recorded phone conversations between the two brothers. Tim and Will apparently suspected that the police may be on to them because they spoke in a code during their recorded conversations. Many amateur criminals believe that using code words during a phone conversation will impede a police investigation and make prosecution difficult or impossible, but even professional criminals have been sunk by carefully coded phone conversations. One of the major pieces of evidence used against mafia kingpin John Gotti during his trial was a series of phone calls where the dialogue was spoken in code. Experts were able to quickly crack the code, which helped send Gotti to prison for the rest of his life.

But Tim and Will Rempel were no John Gottis!

The code the two brothers used was easily cracked by the Calgary police. One particularly damning conversation clearly had to do with the site where Ryan Lane's body was burned.

"They found the kitchen," Will told Tim after the police discovered Ryan's charred remains. "But as hot as it was, there was no DNA."

The mountain of evidence led the jury to quickly convict all three defendants of first degree murder on April 20, 2016. Even Sheena Cuthill, who testified against her cohorts, could not escape the fate she created for herself. The three killers were given life sentences and will not be eligible for parole for twenty-five years.

CHAPTER 5:
The Torture and Murder of Junko Furuta

Modern Japan is a country that is as peaceful as it is beautiful. The large cities are neat, orderly, and clean and the rural areas are dotted with Buddhist and Shinto temples that add a sense of charm and spirituality to the country. Japan is also known for its extremely low crime rate. Gun crime is nearly unheard of and the types of violent crimes that plague cities in most industrialized countries are rare.

Because of the overall nature of contemporary Japanese society, the next crime profiled in this book shocked not only Japan, but the entire world.

In November 1988, sixteen-year-old high school student Junko Furuta was kidnapped from a Tokyo street in broad daylight and then subjected to weeks of torture before she was murdered. Once the perpetrators were caught, the extent of just how horrific and barbaric the crime was came to light.

In particular, the case was notable for the degree of cruelty the killers showed toward their victim. It was truly a case of "man's inhumanity to man" as the murderers relished the pain they inflicted on Junko. And adding to the sheer level of barbarity of the crime itself was the fact that all of the killers were juveniles.

How could children act in such a depraved manner?

Junko's murder made many in Japan realize that their peaceful nation could not totally escape problems experienced by the rest of the world. The case became a media sensation in the Asian nation and brought to the forefront of public discourse issues such as juvenile crime and how society should deal with the worst offenders.

The Abduction

On November 25, 1988, Junko Furuta was a cute, bright, sixteen-year-old student at Yashio-Minami High School in the Tokyo suburb of Misato. Junko was a good student who looked forward to moving on to college and life afterwards. In fact, Junko had just turned sixteen when her life was tragically changed.

After school let out and Junko said goodbye to her friends, she walked down the street to go home, but a van pulled up next to her, opened its side panel door, and two boys snatched her off the street in broad daylight.

The boys did not kill Junko then and there; that would have been merciful. Instead, Junko's journey through hell had just begun.

Three of the boys who abducted Junko began to pummel her with their fists and feet as the fourth one drove the van through the crowded streets of Tokyo to their hideout in the Ayase district of Tokyo. But this was no ordinary hideout; it was the home that one of the abductors, a man now known as Jo Kamisaku, lived in with his parents.

Once the abductors arrived at Kamisaku's home, they quickly hurried their victim to the basement, away from the parents. The boys then covered their tracks by making Junko call her parents, telling them that she was staying at a friend's house for a few days.

It would be the last time Junko spoke with her parents.

Being outnumbered and perhaps believing the boys that she would only be gone for a few days, Junko complied with her abductors.

But the days quickly turned to weeks.

The sadistic boys raped and tortured their helpless victim for a total of forty-four days. At first the boys tried to hide their deed from Kamisaku's parents, but they were unable to do so as Junko screamed with pain during their torture sessions. According to courtroom testimony, Junko even made contact with the parents and pleaded with them for her life, but it was to no avail.

The parents later claimed in court that they were afraid of their son because he repeatedly acted violently towards them and was believed to have connections to the Yakuza. The cowardly nature of the parents was one of many unbelievable aspects of this case.

The parents could have called the police at any time during the forty-four days to end Junko's plight.

And Junko's plight was truly unimaginable.

The boys took turns beating Junko with an iron bar and when they tired of that they poured lighter fluid on her and lit it. They would then take turns raping her and when they tired of that they shoved fireworks and light bulbs into her orifices. Junko repeatedly passed out from the pain of her torture sessions, so in order to revive their victim the boys would burn her with cigarettes.

Truly, there was no limit to the depravity the boys inflicted on poor Junko.

Junko was deprived of proper food and water during her captivity and was instead forced to eat cockroaches and other bugs the sadists found crawling around the basement. For water they forced her to drink her own urine.

Towards the end of the ordeal, Junko was begging to be killed quickly, but unfortunately the sadistic teenagers were not done having their fun. They tied a cord around her neck, hung her from a pipe, and then used her for a punching bag.

Despite the immense physical and psychological torture that Junko endured during her captivity, she attempted to escape on more than one occasion and even made it to a phone in the upstairs.

But one of the boys captured and subjected her to another round of torture.

On January 4, 1989 Junko Furuta finally succumbed to her injuries and died of shock.

Medical experts were actually amazed that she lived as long as she did, having been deprived of proper food and water and suffering massive internal injuries from repeated beatings. After Junko was dead, none of the boys expressed any remorse for what they had done. Instead, their energies turned from torture to figuring out how to cover up their heinous crime.

When the sadistic juveniles learned that their quarry was dead, they put their limited brains together to come up with a disposal method. The solution they conjured up demonstrated their lack of intelligence and maturity, which ultimately led to their swift capture.

The gang placed Junko's body in an oil drum and then poured in wet concrete. They then left the drum in a vacant factory near the waterfront. It did not take the police very long to find the drum after a concerned witness called in a tip. After Junko was taken out of the concrete filled drum, the case became a headliner grabber throughout Japan and became known as the "concrete-encased high school girl murder case."

An Adult Crime but Juvenile Time

The four killers were quickly arrested, not due to forensic evidence or one of the boys developing a guilty conscience, but because there were actually other boys who witnessed part of Junko's ordeal. Early in the kidnapping, there were a few other boys who were present in Kamisaku's home and knew about what was happening to Junko Furuta. Although these other boys claimed to police that they did nothing to the innocent sixteen-year-old, they, like Kamisaku's parents, also did nothing to help her.

The case immediately grabbed headlines in Japan and throughout the world for a number of reasons. The extreme brutality exhibited by the killers and the lack of empathy they showed their victim is shocking in any country, by any standards, but when those details were juxtaposed with the generally peaceful and polite nature of Japanese society it became difficult for many to reconcile. The fact that the victim was a sweet, innocent girl and the nature of her abduction—in broad daylight near her school—was enough to inspire fear in the hearts of many Japanese parents.

But once the disturbing details of the case were made public, most people's concerns turned to the Japanese justice system and how it was so unprepared to deal with such a situation.

The four juvenile sadists were tried as adults, but had their identities sealed. Since the crime rate in Japan is very low, there is no death penalty and even the worst of all murderers usually are released from prison after only serving a few years.

The four boys decided not to try their luck with a trial and instead pled guilty to the murder and hoped to receive lenient sentences. The boys were given sentences that ranged from just a couple of years to about ten years.

The public and Junko's family were outraged at the short length of the sentences.

And for some reason three of the four boys also believed that the Japanese legal system did not treat them fairly so they appealed to have their sentences reduced!

When the appeals of three of Junko's killers made their way to the desk of Judge Ryuji Yanse, he apparently felt the same as many did throughout Japan. Instead of reducing their sentences, Yanse resentenced the leader to twenty-one years in prison and the other two to five to nine and five to seven year sentences.

Jo Kamisaku never appealed his sentence and served eight years total, mainly in a juvenile facility, but the last year of his sentence was spent in an adult prison. All men involved in the horrific murder of Junko Furuta have since been released. Little is known about how the men spent their time in prison, but they were most likely not victimized behind bars. In an American prison system and in probably most other countries around the world for that matter, such inmates would be ostracized by others and left to be victimized by the inmate gangs and stronger, more street-smart convicts. Japanese prisons are quite the opposite. The guards maintain strict control at all times and the inmates are forced to keep silent and meditate most of the day.

With all their time to meditate, one wonders if any of the four felt even a tinge of remorse for Junko.

Jo Kamisaku did not.

After Kamisaku was released in 1999, he took the surname of one of his supporters. He even found middle-class employment at a tech firm and to those who knew him and his past it seemed as though he was truly reformed.

But leave someone to his own devices long enough and he will show you his true character.

In 2004, Kamisaku got into a heated disagreement with an acquaintance over a woman. As the two men exchanged words, Kamisaku threatened the man's life and bragged how he had killed before—he was one of the killers of the girl encased in the concrete. The man was stunned by the allegation, but refused to relent, so Kamisaku attacked him.

The attack left the man in the hospital and Kamisaku with a seven year prison sentence.

The Aftermath

The kidnapping and murder of Junko Furuta left an indelible mark, a deep scar, on the psyche of the Japanese people. The case was tried in the media just as much as in the courtroom, which made it the biggest criminal case in modern Japanese history. It brought ideas of crime and punishment, particularly in regards to juveniles, to the forefront of the public discourse, which until that time had been given little attention and was considered a taboo public topic by many.

The Japanese media also found ways to exploit Junko's murder for profit.

Many books were written and films were produced about the case. A couple of the books were more academic in nature and explored the reasons why young men would commit such a crime, but most of the written material published was of a more popular and sensationalistic nature.

It seems the Japanese learned from the Americans how to profit from crime!

One of the better known films produced about the Junko Furuta murder is titled in English, *The Concrete-Encased High School Murder Case*. The movie is a 1995 exploitation film directed by Katsya Matsumura, who is a legend in the genre of Japanese exploitation films. It is a graphic interpretation of the crime that some think glorifies the sadists to a certain degree.

As books and films were being made about Junko's terrible ordeal, her family was quietly forgotten by most in Japan, which does not mean they did not try to make their voices heard. They voiced their anger to the press over what they and many considered light sentences for their daughter's killers and later won a civil lawsuit against Kamisaku's parents.

But no matter how much money they were awarded, it will never erase the forty-four days of hell that Junko endured at the hands of four sadistic teens.

CHAPTER 6:
Christian Dornier's Rural French Massacre

The recent terrorist attack at Bastille Day festivities in Nice, France, shocked the world and demonstrated how vulnerable public gatherings can be. For many, it forever darkened with blood a day that is usually reserved for revelry, making it impossible for many to enjoy future celebrations on July 14.

But many French citizens who are old enough will tell you that the Nice attack was not the first time Bastille Day celebrations were interrupted because of violence.

Before the 2016 Bastille Day terrorist attacks, France endured a massacre just two days before the national holiday in 1989; but the perpetrator was not a foreign born terrorist with extremist views. He was an average Frenchman who snapped and killed fourteen people.

The shooter was a thirty-one-year old farmer named Christian Dornier who woke up on the morning of July 12, 1989 with one purpose—to paint the streets of the tiny village of Luxiol with the blood of its citizens!

By the time Dornier's murder spree was over, fourteen people were dead and eight more were wounded from gunshots. Dornier's massacre shook the sense of security of the people in a region that was quite familiar with guns, but not gun violence.

Luxiol, which is located about 270 miles northeast of Paris near the Swiss border, could be the picture on a postcard with its bucolic, idyllic setting. Nestled between fields and farms, the village only has about 140 inhabitants and at least as many guns.

Although few countries afford their citizens a constitutional right to bear arms as the United States does, a quick examination reveals that gun laws run on a continuum around the world. Even in Europe, gun laws are not uniform and go from the extremely restrictive, such as in the United Kingdom, to fairly lax and not unlike American laws as can be witnessed in Switzerland.

France has traditionally fit somewhere in the middle of the continuum. Since it is a country with large rural areas and a substantial population of farmers—it is one of the only nation-states in the world with the ability to feed its own population—France has traditionally allowed its rural inhabitants to keep shotguns and some rifles. Handguns and some high powered rifles are more difficult to obtain, but the government has generally taken a lax attitude towards its farmers possessing firearms.

But the Christian Dornier case was just as much about France's mental health industry as it was about the nation's rural gun culture because Dornier showed all the signs of being mentally unhinged before the killing spree.

Christian Dornier

Christian Dornier was born on July 12, 1958, to farmer Georges Dornier and his wife Jeanne. Christian and his younger brother and sister spent most of their time around the family farm when they were not in school. Like most farm kids, Christian and his siblings helped with chores around the farm before and after school, so their lives were busy. With that said, although a lot was expected from the Dornier children, the parents always provided for their children and there were no reports of abuse in the home.

After graduating from high school, Christian did a brief stint in the French army as a conscript. He was discharged honorably from the military, but family and friends said that when Christian returned home he was not the same.

Although as a boy Christian was always a bit shy, after his military service he turned into even more of a recluse and became a true loner. He preferred being alone to the company of others and spent most of his free time either reading or hiking in the local forests.

He had no friends and never dated.

"He had no friends, hardly ever talked to anybody," said his brother Serge just after the massacre. "We knew he was going to create havoc one day and the police should have dealt with him."

As they say though, "hindsight is 20/20", so it is difficult to place blame in such a matter afterwards.

Or is it?

As Christian spent his days in the forests or between the covers of a book, his father was getting older and began to think about the future of the family farm. Instead of selling the farm to a neighbor, Georges decided that he would follow tradition and cede the farm over to his oldest son upon his death, which would be contingent upon Christian learning the trade.

At first Christian seemed to be willing to prove himself to his father. He began taking farming classes at the local vocational college, but quit after a couple of weeks and then became even more withdrawn than before. Seeing that his oldest son was not up to the responsibility of running the family farm, Georges took Christian's name out of the will.

When Christian learned that he would not inherit the family farm, he sulked rather than confront his father on the matter. Throughout his life, Christian was decidedly a passive-aggressive type personality. He rarely argued with individuals, but he was also known to explode with anger in certain situations.

The first months of 1989 witnessed a dramatic and violent turn in Christian's personality.

He was picked up by the police for an incident in which he threw some rocks at a local woman. In the small town where everyone knew each other, including the police, Christian's parents were simply alerted to the incident.

But the rock throwing was not a simple incident.

Christian then brought his violence to the next level.

The recluse took the Dornier family's shotgun and fired a shot at Georges and another one at their neighbor. It is not known if Christian was trying to hit either of the men and missed, or if he was trying to scare them, or if it was to get attention. He succeeded on both counts, as the two frightened men called the local police on the disturbed Christian once more. Unlike the rock throwing incident where Christian was picked up and released to his family, the courts became involved. Although Christian was allowed to return to his family's home, he was ordered to see a psychiatrist.

At first, the visits to the psychiatrist seemed to have helped Christian, but he carried a rage that could not be quenched by a few visits to a shrink.

When Christian's sister Corrine was married on July 8, he was the only immediate family member not in attendance. Instead, Christian spent the day driving back and forth through the village in his Volkswagen Golf. Perhaps he was trying to exorcise his demons or maybe he was going through a dry run of his massacre.

The Massacre

July 12, 1989 began like a normal day for the residents of Luxiol. Some people got up early to take care of their chores, while others began their preparations for Bastille Day, which was only two days away. The residents were happy and content.

They did not know what was in store for them.

For most people a birthday is a day to celebrate with family and close friends, but for Christian Dornier, July 12, his birthday, would be the day when he went to war against the world.

Christian slept late on his birthday and refused to have lunch with his family. Just after lunch the French spree killer would begin his reign of carnage, but he first needed a weapon. After he and the neighbor were shot at by Christian, Georges made sure to hide all of the family's guns in secure locations—except for one.

When Christian learned that his father was hiding all of the family's firearms, he managed to hide one himself in the kitchen.

Christian Dornier would need only one gun.

Just before 2:30 pm Christian moved his brother-in-law's car so that he could later move his VW out of the driveway. He then calmly went back into the kitchen and waited.

At 2:30 he heard a car door slam in the driveway, which he believed was his brother Serge. As soon as the front door of the house began to open, Dornier let loose with the first homicidal shot from his shotgun. His victim fell to the ground instantly, dead.

It was not his brother Serge whom Christian had just killed, but a cattle inseminator named Marcel Lechine. Despite not hitting his intended target, Dornier did not hesitate and turned the gun and shot and killed his sister at point blank range. He then shot his sixty-three-year-old father in the neck, wounding him.

In the confusion of the initial shooting spate in the kitchen, Georges was able to run from the house to a neighbor's for help. Georges yelled for help as he ran to the neighbor's door, confused and bleeding.

Georges' cries for help went unheeded though as his son recovered his bearings, chased him down, and killed him with a single shot to the back.

After dispatching his father, Christian then returned to the Dornier home where he found his mother on the phone with the police. Coldly and without any words, Christian raised the shotgun and fired once, killing his mother.

"There was no argument or quarrel of any kind," said Serge later about his brother's murders of their family members. "He just picked up his gun and fired it point blank at Corinne, killing her instantly. Then my mother telephoned the police . . . He fired and killed her too."

Many people who kill their family members in similar situations often stop there and turn the gun on themselves. But Christian Dornier hated the entire world and wanted everyone to pay for his miserable life, so he was not going to stop until someone made him.

After killing everyone he came in contact with at the Dornier home, Christian reloaded his gun and jumped into his car.

It was time to take his killing spree on the road.

Dornier drove his VW to Luxiol's city center to find some more victims. Almost immediately he came upon two young boys riding their bicycles around town, brothers Johan and Johnny Robez-Masson. He opened fire on the brothers, killing both instantly. He then drove a little further until he spotted Stanislas Pénard and his wife Marie strolling down the sidewalk, enjoying the warm summer day. The young couple never knew what hit them as the farm boy turned spree killer fired buckshot on both, which left them both dead on the street.

As Christian Dornier's body count quickly came to eight, another interesting fact about France's rural gun culture and the reality of gun culture in any country revealed itself.

The presence of more readily available guns may increase the odds of a mass shooting on the one hand, but on the other they can possibly limit the casualties in a mass shooting.

Dornier next shot and killed the mayor's five year-old niece who was standing in front of her home. The girl's father, who was standing nearby, shot back, hitting Dornier in the neck.

Wounded but not done killing, Dornier left Luxiol and drove on to the bigger town of Baume-les-Dames. In Baume-les-Dames, Dornier would claim five more lives, including a policeman named René Sarrazin. By the time Dornier's spree moved to Baume-les-Dames, forty policemen were following him through the town and then across the French countryside as the killer made his way for the town of Verne. Once he arrived in Verne, Dornier was met by even more police who shot him in the stomach, ending his sadistic spree across northeast France.

The final casualty count was fourteen dead, eight seriously wounded.

Insanity Defense

When the smoke finally cleared from Christian Dornier's shooting rampage, the authorities in the region decided to cancel Bastille Day celebrations. The citizens of Luxiol and Baume-les-Dames had wounded to take care of and dead to bury; the national holiday was the furthest thing from the minds of most area residents.

Dornier suffered life threatening injuries and was brought to a secure hospital where doctors fought to save the deranged shooter's life. The French spree killer was saved only to be charged with fourteen counts of murder and eight counts of attempted murder on July 15.

It seemed like an open and shut case for French prosecutors.

Christian Dornier was caught dead to rights. Multiple witnesses saw him at different points during the shooting spree and the farmer turned killer never tried to conceal his face. The French legal system may be thought of as lenient in some ways by American standards, but it was/is not in Europe.

France was one of the last Western European countries to abolish capital punishment. The preferred method of execution in France for over 200 years was the guillotine, which was last used on a criminal in 1977. The French government formally abolished capital punishment in 1981, making it one of the final countries now in the European Union to do so.

So Christian Dornier would not have to face the guillotine, but he very well could have been sent to a prison for the rest of his life.

France has a long history of notorious prisons where famous people, such as American revolutionary Patrick Henry, have languished for years. In more recent years the French government modernized their prison system, but long sentences are routinely handed down and many of the prisons are known for housing tough criminals and inmate gangs.

Christian Dornier would be a sitting duck in a French maximum security prison.

Dornier's defense attorneys knew that he would never be truly safe in a maximum security prison and that when, not if, he were convicted of the murders, he would be sent to such a prison for the remainder of his life.

They decided to try an insanity defense.

Attempts at insanity defenses are actually common during murder trials. A defendant with enough money will locate and pay mental health professionals who will testify that the defendant was insane when he/she committed the murder. Because of the possibility to abuse such a defense, most countries require an extremely high standard for someone to prove he/she was insane during the commission of a murder. The process involves separate hearings and the end result is that the judge usually rules the defendant competent to stand trial.

But sometimes the courts rule in favor of a defendant's insanity plea.

Investigators soon learned that Christian Dornier did indeed have mental health issues, had been to see a psychiatrist, and was prescribed medication. While Dornier was convalescing from his wounds in the hospital, the government sent its own team of psychiatrists to exam the shooter in order to determine if he could stand trial.

The psychiatrists reported that Christian Dornier suffered from schizophrenia and that he should not be held legally responsible for the July 12, 1989, rampage. Due to the findings, the French government sent Dornier to a state mental hospital on April 18, 1991, where he remains to this day.

Over the last twenty-five years, numerous petitions have been filed to have Dornier declared competent to stand trial in a criminal court; but all have been denied.

Christian Dornier's shooting spree truly upset the tranquility of the otherwise quiet French countryside. The rampage was the worst shooting in French history since a 1978 gangland shooting left ten people dead in Marseilles.

It took more than twenty-five years, but Dornier's carnage count was finally eclipsed by the November 2015 Paris terrorist attacks that left 130 people dead, over half from gunshots.

But the citizens of the quiet villages of northeast France will never forget Christian Dornier's shooting rampage.

CHAPTER 7:
The Mysterious Murder of Jessica Lynn Keen

As discussed in an earlier chapter in this book, rebellion is a part of growing up and being a teenager. Most pass through the phase quickly and then move on with their lives. When most of us look back on our teen years, we often laugh at some of the things we did, while others may want to forget most of it.

Teen rebellion is handled by parents in a variety of different ways. Some parents give their insubordinate adolescents plenty of leeway, while others come down strongly on their recalcitrant kids. Parenting is not a "one size fits all" proposition and the best results seem to come from a variety of different methods.

But sometimes, no matter what a parent does, the worst case scenario will unfortunately happen.

A Good Girl Gone Bad

In 1991, Jessica Keen was a girl whose life took an interesting, difficult, and unexpected arc in her fifteen short years of life.

Jessica Keen grew up in the Weiland Park neighborhood of Columbus, Ohio, which is situated between the campus of Ohio State University and downtown Columbus. The neighborhood was fairly safe for a big city and she lived in a stable home. Her mother and father were married and living together and there was no abuse, drug use, or criminal activity taking place in the home.

Jessica got along well with her family and was popular at her high school. Her popularity in school translated into her being one of the top cheerleaders, but Jessica also excelled in academics and was an honor student. Jessica looked set to receive a scholarship from Ohio State University, or perhaps any number of universities.

But then eighteen-year-old bad boy Shawn Thompson came along.

The Keen parents immediately disliked Thompson, who they saw as lazy, shiftless, and lacking in any future. Thompson was also rumored to be involved in criminal activity in the area.

As Jessica's grades began to decline, the Keens' disapproval of their daughter's boyfriend became more adamant. They forbade her from seeing Thompson and then grounded her when she disobeyed them. Finally, feeling they were at their wit's end, the Keen parents made the drastic decision to send Jessica to a group home for troubled teens.

Jessica was sent to live in a nearby group home named the Huckleberry House on March 4, 1991. Her parents hoped that the exile would help to refocus Jessica on school and the future and if Thompson was unable to see her, so much the better.

Instead of helping their daughter, Jessica's sojourn to the group home proved to be her demise in a strange series of events that was only recently solved by modern science.

Jessica's Murder

On March 17, 1991, less than two weeks after she was sent to Huckleberry House, the naked body of Jessica Keen was discovered in a cemetery just outside of Columbus. The police quickly amassed a trail of physical evidence that painted a graphic image of Jessica's last minutes on earth.

Due to her naked body and duct tape on her hands and mouth, it became clear that Jessica had been abducted at some point on March 17. An autopsy revealed that she had been raped and beaten to death. A pendant she wore of the word "taken" was missing, but her watch and ring were left by the killer.

Investigators found one of Jessica's socks behind one gravestone and a knee imprint behind another. It became clear to homicide detectives that she escaped her attacker at some point and ironically, ran into the cemetery for refuge. She moved through the cemetery, hiding behind gravestones, until her devious killer finally caught her on the edge of the cemetery, which proved to be Jessica's final resting place.

The Keen family was mortified when they learned about Jessica's murder and the city of Columbus went into high alert when it was informed that a killer-rapist was roaming the streets freely.

The police quickly had a prime suspect—Jessica's boyfriend, Shawn Thompson

When investigators interviewed the staff and residents of the Huckleberry House, they learned that Jessica and Shawn had an argument on the phone on the night of March 17. After the phone call, Jessica signed out of the Huckleberry House around six pm and was never seen nor heard from again.

The Keen family and many in the city of Columbus thought that Shawn Thompson was good for the murder, but it was soon revealed that he could not have been the perpetrator. Thompson had witnesses who claimed he was on the way to Florida with them during the murder and DNA profiling, which still was still relatively new in the early 1990s, eventually proved him innocent.

Once Shawn Thompson was definitively ruled out as a suspect, the only thing left for the police to do was to store the biological evidence from the crime scene and hope that science would one day catch the killer.

Modern Science Reveals the Killer

As the 1990s started to go by, the parents of Jessica Keen and many of the investigators involved in her case began to lose hope that they would catch her killer. The young girl's brutal murder began to be featured less in local media stories, which was not due to her family's efforts. They routinely checked in with the local police and reporters in order to keep the case from going cold and to keep it in the minds of the public. Jessica's family's efforts were enough to get the case profiled on the popular American true-crime television show *Unsolved Mysteries* and was featured on an episode of *On the Case with Paula Zahn*. Despite these efforts, it looked to many as though Jessica's killer would never be caught.

In the years since Jessica's murder, the science of DNA profiling advanced rapidly.

The biological samples taken from Jessica's body were preserved in a crime lab and then entered into the Combined DNA Index System (CODIS) when Ohio became part of the database in the 2000s. When Congress passed the DNA Identification Act in 1994, it cleared the way for the creation of a nationwide DNA base of convicted criminals. Although CODIS is an FBI program, samples are taken from offenders in all fifty states, the federal government, and the District of Colombia. At first, samples were taken from convicted sex offenders in various states, but over the years the database has grown to include persons convicted of all felonies and in some states, those even charged with felonies and some misdemeanors. Each individual state determines its own criteria for who is required to give DNA samples, but by 2006 every state had joined the CODIS database on some level.

Columbus police suspected that whoever killed Jessica had either committed a serious crime before, or would again at some point. In 2008 the investigators theory proved to be true when they received a match in the CODIS system for the semen left on Jessica's body.

The sample belonged to a man named Marvin Lee Smith Junior. It was immediately clear that Smith's sample was no fluke: he was a career criminal who was out on bond for sexually assaulting two Columbus women when Jessica was murdered. On April 9, 2008, Columbus police traveled to North Carolina and arrested Smith for the murder of Jessica.

Once Smith was extradited to Ohio to stand trial for capital murder in 2009, he showed his cowardly nature by pleading guilty to the murder in order to avoid the death penalty. As part of a plea bargain that got him a life sentence instead of the needle, Smith was required to tell the court what happened the night of Jessica's murder.

Coming off the previous two sexual assaults, the depraved Smith was driven to rape again, but this time he had to make sure his victim could not go to the police. As he drove around Columbus looking for his next victim, he spied Jessica waiting alone at a bus stop. Like a true predator, Smith pulled up next to Jessica, assaulted her, and then threw her into his car. He then bound her with duct tape and raped the frightened girl. Jessica apparently knew that her attacker had no plans to let her live, so she ran from the car into the cemetery. Smith admitted that he had a difficult time finding her in the graveyard, but he was helped when Jessica unwittingly ran into a fencepost, which knocked her unconscious.

The killer then finished Jessica off by smashing a tombstone over her head.

The cold irony of being murdered in a cemetery is something that is difficult to contemplate and will always live with Jessica's parents.

"I can still feel Jessica's heart beating as she ran for her life that day," said Jessica's mother, Rebecca Smitley. "I can see her hiding behind tombstones and I can hear her praying.

CHAPTER 8:
Mattias Flink's Swedish Shooting Spree

Since the 1970s, the focus of the justice system in most industrialized countries has been to rehabilitate, instead of just punishing criminals, or at least that is what is said. Prisons and jails in many countries offer classes to inmates ranging from parenting to vocational and college courses that are aimed at helping inmates find jobs after they are released.

The old days of locking someone up and throwing away the keys are long over.

Despite the emphasis on rehabilitation over punishment, modern justice systems still function to punish those who have ran afoul of society's laws. The very act of separating a person from his family, friends, and greater society is an act of punishment and few will argue that in countries that still have the death penalty, the execution of a criminal is an act of revenge on behalf of the victims' families and society itself.

Lengthy prison sentences handed out to murderers are viewed by most as the proper course for a person who has committed the ultimate crime. Proponents of long prison sentences argue that such sentences protect society from convicted murderers, who may kill again, and also serve to punish the most heinous offenders.

But how does society determine if a killer is truly reformed? Even if a killer is said to be reformed, should he continue to be held as punishment for his crime(s) as revenge for the victims?

These are common questions that are often bandied about by legal scholars who seek to create the most fair justice system. In the United States, convicted murderers usually serve very long prison sentences for one murder and it is unheard for a spree or serial killer to ever obtain parole.

Things are a bit different in Scandinavia.

Since crime is relatively low in the Scandinavian countries, their justice systems have funding for more expansive inmate rehabilitation programs. The prisons in Norway, Sweden, and Denmark, are viewed by many in corrections as models for the industrialized world and sentencing for crimes is often creative and lenient, at least by American standards.

For instance, a true life sentence is unheard of in most Scandinavian countries. This point was particularly made clear to the world when Norwegian terrorist Anders Breivik was sentenced to twenty-one years "preventive detention" in Norway for his attack that left seventy seven people dead and over 300 wounded. Under the law, the government can imprison Breivik indefinitely, but he will also be eligible for parole after ten years.

Most experts say the chance that Breivik will ever be released are remote, but one only has to look at neighboring Sweden and the case of Mattias Flink to know that when it comes to remote probabilities in Scandinavian justice systems, one should not discount anything.

Mattias Flink killed seven people and injured one in what many consider to be Sweden's worst crime.

The convicted spree killer was recently released from prison!

The Mattias Flink murder spree raised alarms and anger in the liberal, peaceful Nordic nation that had not witnessed that type of violence since the Vikings made Scandinavia their home. A frenzy of media attention gripped Sweden in the months following Flink's murder spree in 1994 and years later when the case became the center of attention again as Flink fought to be released from prison.

Mattias Flink

Mattias Flink was born on March 8, 1970, to a middle-class family in the small central Swedish town of Falun. From an early age Flink was surrounded by guns because his father worked as a gunsmith. Although handguns are severely restricted in Sweden, rifles and shotguns are quite common and the country is usually in the ten top of the countries with the most guns per 100 residents.

Mattias' father showed him how to properly care for and maintain firearms around the house and the two would also often do target practice together.

The Flink home was stable; the father earned enough to support the small family and there was no abuse. Despite the early stability of the Flink home, his parents came under the same stresses that most families experience in modern industrialized countries, which ended in divorce when Mattias was nine.

Psychiatrists point to his parents' divorce as an early traumatic and defining experience in Mattias Flink's life.

After the divorce was finalized, young Mattias stayed in the family home with his father while his mother moved down the street. He began to resent his mother for the divorce.

He began to resent women for everything!

For the most part, Flink's youth was rather non-descript. He had few friends and spent most of his time around the family home until he graduated from high school and then joined the Swedish army.

Army life seemed to agree with Flink as it gave him some things that were otherwise missing in his life. The rules gave him order, discipline, and direction that were not there before and although he still maintained a reasonable personal distance from the other soldiers, he did develop a sense of comradery with officers and enlisted men alike.

Flink's dedication to military life eventually paid off when he was promoted the rank of Second Lieutenant. It looked to many of Flink's family and long-time friends that the young man had finally found his place in life and was truly happy.

Looks can be deceiving.

The entire time that Flink was being promoted through the ranks of the Swedish military, his hatred for the world kept festering. Although he had a girlfriend in 1994, Flink increasingly began to shut her and all of his other acquaintances out from his inner circle that only included Mattias Flink.

In the first couple months of 1994 Flink also began drinking heavily. The drinking combined with his misanthropic nature led to him acting aggressively on numerous occasions towards friends and acquaintances, as he accused them of conspiring against him.

The signs were all there: heavy drinking, isolation, and paranoia; but no one, including his superiors at the army base, believed there was a problem.

They would all soon find out just how much of a problem Mattias Flink could be!

Washing Falun in Blood

Falun is a sleepy college town of about 40,000 people located in the central part of Sweden. Once one of the of primary producers of iron and copper in Europe, by early 1994 more of Falun's residents were employed in the educational, recreational, and military sectors than in mining.

The military presence in Falun was barely considered by the local residents before 1994, partly because it had been there so long, but also because incidents of criminal behavior that have a tendency to follow military bases were for the most part absent.

Until June 11, 1994.

June 11 began like many other days for Mattias Flink. It was just another day—another day for him to hate the world. But unlike those other days, Flink would do something about it on this day.

Flink began the day drinking copious amounts of hard liquor, which only served to harden his already negative disposition. At some point during his drinking binge, Flink began to argue with his girlfriend. The argument seemed to flip a switch in Flink's twisted mind, but for some reason he never laid a hand on his girlfriend.

Perhaps he wanted her to see the carnage that he was capable of.

Flink finished of a bottle of vodka, got dressed, and then loaded his military issued AK 5 rifle.

He then headed for the park to hunt his game—women!

Flink could not have picked a better time to hunt women in Fulan because when he arrived at the park, a squad of the Sweden Women's Auxiliary Service was conducting drills. Eyeing up his hated quarry, Flink fired several shots from his high-powered rifle into the crowd of women, killing five and injuring one.

Flink then surveyed the situation and noticed a man on a bicycle had just witnessed the shooting, so he shot and killed him. An unarmed security guard who was on duty nearby ran to the vicinity to help out, but he was also shot and killed by the woman-hating gunman.

With eight bullet-ridden bodies strewn across the park, Flink then ran from the area to a nearby construction site to hide.

It is unknown if Flink was seriously trying to hide from the police or if he was merely catching his breath before he killed more people: he left his house with 150 rounds of ammo and barely used any of them during his proficient killing spree in the park. But the local police were on high alert and soon two officers spotted Flink in his makeshift hideout. A shootout ensued that left Flink with a bullet in the hip and in handcuffs.

The killing spree in Falun was over, but the legal saga of Mattias Flink had just begun.

Life In and Out of Prison

Perhaps "saga" is the most appropriate word in this case and best sums up the trial, conviction, imprisonment, and eventual release of Mattias Flink. Saga is after all an Old Norse word for the stories about the Viking kings and jarls who at one time ruled over Sweden. Most sagas followed a standard formula: the protagonist loses his birthright for some reason and is then forced to endure tribulations before returning home and claiming what is rightfully his, usually through acts of extreme violence. Now Flink never had any claim to nobility and the tribulations he endured were largely the result of mental health issues, but the legal maneuvering connected to his trial and imprisonment represent a saga of a different sort.

Flink was immediately charged with murder in a case that was sensationalized in the Swedish media, but it was also a case that most saw as open and shut. Plenty of witnesses saw Flink shoot numerous people and then there was that shootout he got into with the police.

But never underestimate a good defense lawyer!

At first, it seemed as though Sweden's low crime rate might work to Flink's advantage because his attorneys were able to use a defense that was previously unknown in Sweden—not guilty due to an alcohol induced psychosis.

The defense that "alcohol made me do it" may seem laughable today, but in 1994 Flink's lawyers considered it a legitimate defense. Low crime rates and a liberal justice system meant that Swedish judges and juries were more apt to consider such a defense as opposed to their American counterparts who are more cynical due to high crime rates.

After all, a nice solider like Mattias Flink certainly had to be out of his mind to commit such terrible crimes, right?

Despite well-reasoned arguments by the defense, the court rejected Flink's claims of insanity by the bottle and found him guilty of murder. Not only was Flink's booze defense rejected in his trial, it created a nationwide precedent so that criminal defendants cannot use the "so drunk I'm insane" defense in Sweden today.

Once Flink was convicted and sentenced to life in prison, the people of Sweden thought they had heard the last of the butcher of Falun. Little did they know that it was really just the beginning of the next chapter in the saga of Mattias Flink.

Like most people serving an extended sentence behind bars, Flink was moved to a couple of different prisons. For the most part, he was well behaved, but he kept to himself. Because of a combination of his misanthropic attitude and the notoriety of his crime, Flink was unpopular with the other inmates. Despite the other inmates' hatred of Flink, he was able to avoid any serious assaults at their hands.

Flink put his solitude behind bars to good use.

The spree killer took part in prison rehabilitation programs and showed enough promise to prison staff that he was allowed furloughs starting in 2007, despite serving a life sentence. The shooter of Falun also used his time to study Swedish law and legal procedures and learned that he had an outside chance of reducing his sentence.

Beginning in 2008, Flink filed numerous appeals with the courts to have his sentence reduced from life to twenty-four years. Once the media learned of Flink's legal maneuvering, the rampage in Falun became headlines once more and the people of Sweden became outraged that such a heinous killer may once again roam their streets.

In 2010, the Norns began to favor Flink in a series of court rulings. An appeals court agreed to reduce Flink's sentence to thirty-two years, but then a subsequent ruling handed him thirty-six years. Finally, Sweden's Supreme Court handed Flink an adjusted sentence of thirty years, which gave the spree killer a parole date of June 11, 2014, exactly twenty years after he gunned down seven people in Falun.

Since his release from prison, Flink's identity and location have been kept secret from the public. It remains to be seen if Flink was truly rehabilitated by his prison experience; perhaps he got the help he needed. To many of the family members of Flink's victims the question of his rehabilitation is a moot point. To victims' families, he should stay in prison for the rest of his life for punishment, if nothing else.

Only time will tell what happens next.

Is there another chapter waiting to be written in the strange saga of Mattias Flink?

CHAPTER 9:
Matthew Tvrdon's White Van Rampage

In recent years, automobiles have been used quite frequently around the world as weapons. One does not have to search the Internet very long to find examples of this. The 2002 case of Clara Harris repeatedly running over her husband in a parking lot is one of the more striking cases. As in the Clara Harris case, most automobile homicides are very personal and directed at only one or two people, so the casualty count tends to be low.

Make no mistake, an automobile can be just as deadly in the wrong hands as a gun, knife, or bomb.

Unfortunately, the world was starkly shown this reality when a terrorist plowed a truck into a crowd of Bastille Day revelers in Nice, France, killing dozens.

But before the Bastille Day truck attack in Nice, there was Matthew Tvrdon and his white van rampage in Cardiff, Wales!

The Death Van

Wales is an interesting country. A trip through the rural mountain country of Wales will demonstrate to anyone that despite being a part of the United Kingdom, Wales is indeed a unique place. Many of the people still speak their native Welsh language and the names of the country's cities, lakes, and mountains also retain their incredibly long and difficult to pronounce Welsh names, although many locals admit that it would be easier to use English names. Despite holding strong to their cultural traditions, most Welsh are happy being part of the Kingdom and do not display the vehement and sometimes violent anti-English attitude often seen in Northern Ireland and Scotland.

Wales is truly a quiet and charming country.

At least it was until twenty-nine-year-old Matthew Tvrdon filled up his van with gas on October 19, 2012 and decided to turn that vehicle into a lethal weapon.

Matthew Tvrdon was an average guy in many ways. He worked an average job at a government tax office, but eventually the stress of dealing with other people's money became too much and he had a nervous breakdown.

Or perhaps there were problems all along.

Tvrdon's behavior at work earned him an extended stay at a Cardiff psychiatric hospital, but he was allowed to return to his job after he was released from the hospital. After his return to work, it soon became apparent to his co-workers that the stay in the hospital did not help and if anything, Tvrdon seemed even more withdrawn.

Most people who knew Tvrdon before his rampage had good things to say about him and one co-worker even stated that their employer "seriously let him down" by not taking his mental health more seriously.

Matthew Tvrdon's neighbors from the neighborhood he grew up in also had good things to say about the killer. He was known to be polite and enjoyed working on cars, either alone or with his father or two younger brothers.

There was no abuse in the Tvrdon home and the parents were not involved in criminal activity, drug use, or heavy drinking. It seemed a mystery how a well-adjusted boy could transform into a mental basket-case by the age of thirty.

Perhaps he was a spurned lover?

Tvrdon was dating an older forty-six-year-old woman in the months before his rampage, but the woman was said to have broken off the relationship. It is unknown what role this may have played, but authorities have down played it.

The world may never know the true intentions of Tvrdon's murderous spree, but the citizens of Cardiff continue to live with its repercussions.

It all began on a Friday afternoon at 3:30 pm. Children had been let out of school and many of their parents were there to pick up them. The streets of Cardiff were alive with the sounds of children laughing.

Within minutes the laughs turned to screams.

After Tvrdon checked his van one last time, he made his way to the Ely and Leckwith districts to find some victims. He did not have to wait long.

Tvrdon immediately went into action, driving his van into groups of adults and children wherever he could find them. He swerved across several lanes of traffic in order to attack one group and then back to the other side of the street to run over a couple who were walking their baby in a stroller.

The psychotic van driver plowed into the couple, thrusting the child several feet into the air. Somehow the child lived!

Tvrdon then drove up the street to a local fire department station where he spied thirty-one-year old mother Karina Menzies and her two children. Menzies, who had problems walking because of a degenerative disease, had her infant with her as she had just picked up her eight-year-old from school. As the white van of death sped towards Menzies, the mother did the only thing possible and threw her two children to safety.

The white van crushed Menzies' body, killing her instantly.

By the time Karina Menzies was killed, Tvrdon had already hit and driven over at least a dozen people, so the police were on their way.

Street-beat cops in the United Kingdom are known world-wide for not carrying firearms, but firearms and other weapons are available if needed.

And the Cardiff police needed some heavy power to take down Matthew Tvrdon!

After Tvrdon killed Menzies, the white van rampage soon turned into a hot pursuit as dozens of local police gave chase to the crazed killer.

Tvrdon led the Cardiff Police on a chase that went for several miles through several neighborhoods and finally ended when the police shot tear gas into the killer's car.

The white van rampage was over.

The Sentence

Once Tvrdon was captured and placed in custody, he faced the anger of a nation and the possibility that he would spend the rest of his life in prison. The case was never a "who done it?" Numerous closed circuit television cameras captured the carnage and were able to corroborate witnesses who saw and survived the mayhem. The real question concerned whether or not Tvrdon was legally responsible for his actions or if he was insane.

After a number of pre-trial hearings intended to determine Tvrdon's sanity, a judge ruled that the killer was not criminally responsible because, like Christian Dornier, he suffered from schizophrenia. In 2013, Tvrdon was then sentenced to an indefinite term at a maximum security mental hospital.

Many of the people at the hearing, who were also survivors of the van attack, became irate and yelled their disapproval of the sentence to the judge, press, and anyone else who would listen. As one man left the courtroom he shouted, "They should have put a gun to his head." Of course the statement was hyperbole and more than likely just a way for a frustrated person to blow off steam since the death penalty was abolished during the 1960s in the United Kingdom.

Despite what many may think, Matthew Tvrdon did not get off lightly.

Experts say that he will probably spend the rest of his life at the Ashworth high-security hospital, which is located in the northwest English town of Merseyside. The hospital is little better than an average British prison in most ways and the "indefinite" sentence does not mean that he will ever be released.

Once the sentence was handed down the judge made sure to add, "However, you should expect that you will be detained for a very long time."

Matthew Tvrdon will most likely never terrorize the streets of Cardiff, or any other city in the United Kingdom.

CHAPTER 10:
The Case of the Real Life Zombie, Tyree Smith

Zombie movies and television shows have become the rage over the last few years. The success of *The Walking Dead* television show has led to numerous imitators on cable television and a plethora of movies and books that are too numerous to count.

Truly, the world has become obsessed with zombies.

For most people, becoming immersed in a world overrun with flesh eating undead creatures is more of an escape from the mundane nature of daily life more than anything else. We find satisfaction when our favorite hero or heroine escapes the clutches of a pack of flesh eaters in the latest episode of our favorite zombie show and we are perhaps even happier to watch the villains eviscerated by zombies. Once the show is over though, it is back to reality and the daily grind.

But some people among us have a desire for human flesh and the most disturbed of those people sometimes act on those desires.

All throughout history there have been reports of people who have broken mankind's biggest taboo—cannibalism. With that said, reports of cannibalism have been rare enough that they are usually well reported and often under understandable circumstances. For instance, Russian civilians who were trapped in Stalingrad during that city's siege by the Germans in late 1942 and early 1943 were said to have survived by eating dead friends and family members. And of course there is the famous case of the Uruguayan rugby team whose plane crashed in the Andes Mountains in 1972. The surviving members of the team were able to survive by eating the bodies of the dead.

Those were true cases of life and death, where the survivors had to eat human flesh and by all accounts found the act extremely difficult.

Then there are truly disturbed people who enjoy eating human flesh, like Ed Gein. Ed Gein made international headlines when it was discovered that the central Wisconsin farmer had killed and eaten some of his neighbors. The world was disturbed that not only was Gein a murderer, but also a cannibal who hid among his neighbors in plain sight.

Nearly sixty years later, a cannibal named Tyree Smith struck on the streets of Bridgeport, Connecticut, raising alarm in the city. Some of the older residents were reminded of the Ed Gein case decades earlier, but most people, influenced by the current zombie rage, saw Smith as a true-to-life zombie.

Eyeballs Taste Like Oysters

In January 2012, thirty-four-year-old Tyree Smith was just another person who fell through the cracks. Smith had spent his life in and out of correctional and mental health facilities and dealing with substance abuse issues. He had a difficult time finding good paying work and when he did find a job he was usually fired fairly quickly. As he got older, Smith became increasingly estranged from his family and was often homeless.

Life had been tough for Tyree Smith.

On January 20, 2012, Smith found himself homeless in the middle of a Connecticut winter and desperately needed a place to stay and keep warm. After searching around the city for a place to crash, Smith found what looked like a vacant house and quickly fell asleep on the porch due to exhaustion.

After sleeping for a couple of hours, Smith was woken up by a man who invited him inside to sleep. The man was not the home's owner; Smith was correct that the house was vacant. The stranger was forty-three-year-old homeless drifter Angel Gonzalez.

There is no evidence that Gonzalez tried to do anything violent to Smith, or that he may made an unwanted sexual advance. It appears that Smith simply snapped in order to satiate his unnatural taste for human flesh.

Not long after moving his things into the house, Smith pulled out an axe and hacked Gonzalez to death. The motiveless murder was bizarre in its own right, but what happened next was just incredibly weird.

Smith surveyed his victim and then proceeded to remove an eyeball and some of the brain matter. He then left the body in the vacant house but took the eyeball and brain matter to a family member's grave at a nearby cemetery. Smith then ate the eyeball, which "tasted like an oyster," according to his arrest warrant. He also chowed down on the brain matter.

Smith then went on the run for a few days but was arrested on January 24 in Florida.

After Smith was extradited back to Connecticut, the details of his bizarre, horrific crime became public.

Smith showed up at the home of his cousin, Nicole Rabb, the day before the murder and zombie feast. Rabb testified that he acted stranger than normal and that he was "talking about Greek gods and ruminating about needing to go out and get blood."

Instead of blood, Smith got an eyeball and some brain matter.

In pre-trial hearings it became obvious to both the defense and prosecutor that Smith was not sane. A three judge panel agreed and declared the zombie killer not guilty by reason of insanity in July 2013. Technically, the ruling meant that the panel could have ordered his immediate release because he was ruled not-guilty.

But the ruling also made Smith a ward of the state until he is deemed no longer a danger to himself or anyone else, so it seems likely that the zombie killer will be spending quite a while, if not the rest of his life, in a state hospital.

"It is overwhelmingly clear that his discharge from custody would constitute a danger to himself and others," stated Superior Court Judge John Kavenewsky as he ordered Smith to sixty years confinement in a secured mental hospital.

Although most in attendance seemed to think that the lengthy confinement in a mental hospital was a fair resolution for the strange crime, some of Gonzalez's family still had a difficult time coming to grips with the bizarre circumstances of Angel's murder.

"Here it is that my dad was trying to help this guy, telling him to come inside from the cold," said Odalys Vazquez, a daughter of Angel Gonzalez. "If my father was helping him stay warm, what kind of person is it who does this—who repays him by swinging an axe at him and hitting him so hard it blows his brains out?"

It was a legitimate question, but the circumstances surrounding this case are just so strange that Tyree Smith himself will probably never be able to answer it, at least not in a way that normal people would understand.

CHAPTER 11:
The Cold Murder Case of Wilhelmina and Ed Maurin

There are usually many reasons why a murder case becomes cold. A lack of physical evidence, motive, or suspects are always problems that can stymie an investigation, but oftentimes there is a lack of will and resources to solve many of these murders. Police departments are forced to budget their resources, which includes manpower, so some cases get temporarily pushed aside while attention is given to more pressing cases. Unfortunately, the cases that are often temporarily pushed aside are usually forgotten about by investigators. The lack of urgency is even more apparent when a considerable amount of time has elapsed since the crime.

Investigators are transferred, promoted, and retire, which means that twenty or thirty years after a murder has been committed and the case has grown cold, there are few if any investigators around who worked on the case originally.

The will to capture the perpetrators of cold case murders often comes from friends and family members of the victims. It is their efforts that keep the cold cases in the public eye through the media, as well as by constantly keeping contact with law enforcement assigned to solve the crimes.

The 1985 cold case murders of eighty-three-year-old Wilhelmina "Winnie" Maurin and her eighty-one-year-old husband Ed is a perfect example of a family member not giving up and ultimately making sure that their murder did not remain cold.

"At their funeral, I laid my hand on their casket," said Dennis Hadaller, the son of Winnie and Ed Maurin. "I said, I will find out who did this."

Eventually, Dennis' persistence paid off—nearly thirty years later—but not before the case took some twists and turns.

A Brutal Murder

Winnie and Ed Maurin were discovered shot to death in the woods outside of Centralia, Washington on Christmas Eve, 1985. The brutality and apparent randomness of the murders perplexed the residents of Lewis County, Washington. Lewis County is predominately rural, has fewer than 100,000 residents, and is known for its low crime rates.

The crime scene, or perhaps dumping scene, indicated that their deaths were no accident. Whoever it was they met up with, that person or persons intended to kill the Maurins.

With plenty of questions, but few leads, the Lewis County Sherriff's Department got to work creating a chronology of the

Maurins' last days alive. They started with the date when the Maurin's were last seen or heard from.

December 19, 1985, was an important date for the Maurin family. That night, the extended Maurin family was supposed to meet at Winnie and Ed's home to celebrate Christmas, but when the guests began to arrive they found the Maurin home locked and totally dark.

Feeling that something was wrong, Dennis and some of his other relatives went to the Lewis County Sherriff's Department to file a missing person report. The Sherriff's department quickly determined that the Maurins were not a couple trying to get lost and that they had both either succumbed to some type of affliction common in old age—Alzheimer's disease, heart attack, or stroke just to name three possibilities—or they met with untimely demises at the hands of others.

An extensive search was conducted throughout Lewis County, which turned up the Maurins' car the next day.

The discovery of the Maurins' car was greeted with optimism by the Maurin family, but that hope soon faded when they learned about the conditions of the interior: the key was still in the ignition and there was a lot of blood on the seats.

So much blood, investigators said, that if it were shed by even two people they most surely died of blood loss. The Maurin family's hopes of finding Winnie and Ed alive sunk and were permanently dashed when the bodies of the elderly couple were discovered on Christmas Eve.

The disappearance of Winnie and Ed Maurin was officially ruled a double homicide and local investigators immediately set to work finding their killers.

But they soon found out how difficult a homicide investigation can be without physical evidence.

Two Suspects Emerge

Smaller law enforcement agencies in the United States, such as the Lewis County Sherriff's Department, are often underfunded and therefore do not often have the latest crime fighting technologies that bigger departments possess. The smaller tax bases in less populated towns and counties is one of the primary reasons these departments have less resources, but these communities also tend to have less of a need because crime rates are traditionally lower in these locations.

And all of the latest technologies would not have helped much anyway.

Investigators were immediately faced with the problem of a lack of physical evidence at the crime scene. Although DNA profiling was unknown in 1985, investigators could test blood for types and the only types they could identify from the car were those that matched Ed's and Winnie's. There were also no fingerprints other than the Maurins in the car or their home. Closed circuit television cameras were a fairly novel concept in 1985 and there were few witnesses that could help investigators, at least in the early stages of the investigation.

Ed Maurin was seen in Chehalis under strange circumstances on the day of the 19th.

The investigators were able to combine the Ed Maurin sighting with tips from informants to not only zero in on two suspects, but also to recreate the horrific crime that took the lives of two innocent people.

In 1985, Rick and John Riffe were a couple of twenty-somethings with no real ambitions or plans for the future. Although the two brothers were known to local law enforcement as bottom of the totem pole criminals, they were not known to have been especially violent or to have committed any major crimes, so they stayed under police radars for the most part.

But when the Lewis County Sherriff's Department began hearing stories that the two were involved in the murder of the Maurins, they began to take notice.

As the police built a case against the two brothers, the Riffes moved up to Alaska. Younger brother John died in 2012, so he evaded justice on this earth, but in 2013 Rick was charged for the murders of Winnie and Ed Maurin.

Behind the efforts to charge the one surviving brother was Dennis Hadaller, who hired a private investigator in the early

2000s. The private investigator revealed new witnesses, which ultimately helped police piece together the crime and charge Rick Riffe with murder.

According to the police and the Lewis County prosecutor's office, the murder of the Maurins was purely financially based. An employee at the Sterling Savings and Loan banks in Chehalis testified that a man whose voice she did not recognize called around closing time on December 18, 1985 and asked if it were too late to withdraw a large sum of cash. The teller told the man to call back the next day.

The mysterious caller never gave his name. The next day the same teller got a call about withdrawing a large sum of cash, but this time it was from a customer she knew: Ed Maurin.

Ed arrived at the bank promptly at 10:30 am on the morning of the 19th and withdrew $8,500 in $100 bills. He told the teller that he needed the money in order to buy a new car. When the teller asked about Winnie, who usually accompanied Ed into the bank, he replied that she was not feeling well and decided to wait in the car. The teller told Ed that they did not have that much money on hand and that he would have to wait for more cash to arrive. Ed decided to wait in his car with his wife.

After Ed finally got his cash, he thanked the teller and told her that he would drive his new car through the drive-up window the next time he came to the bank.

That was the last time Ed was seen alive.

Police theorize that the Riffe brothers had picked the Maurins as marks days or weeks before the homicides were committed. Rick gained entry to the Maurin home in the early morning hours of the 19th and then forced the couple at gunpoint into their 1969 Chrysler. John then joined his brother and the four drove into town together to get Ed's money.

The Maurins' car was spotted several times around town that day, including driving away from the Maurin home with all four occupants.

Based on the autopsy of Ed, one or both of the brothers hit the elderly man at least twice on the top of the head in order to get him to comply. They then threatened to kill Winnie if Ed did not withdraw the money and they waited with her in the car as insurance.

Although robbery was the primary intent of the plot, the Riffe brothers probably intended to kill their marks from the beginning. They were loose ends that needed to be cut.

Dead men tell no tales!

But Rick Riffe learned that although dead men might not be able to tell tales, living witnesses can. Riffe's attorney argued that since his client's fingerprints and DNA were not found at the crime scene, then there was no way a jury could convict beyond a reasonable doubt. He also pointed out that some of the eyewitness testimony conflicted.

But the witnesses whose testimony did not conflict with others were considered credible and the circumstances of the situation proved to be too much. A Lewis County, Washington jury convicted Rick Riffe of murder on November 19, 2013.

Despite a lack of physical evidence, Lewis County Sheriff Steve Mansfield never doubted the Riffe brothers' guilt in the murders.

"I believe in karma, these are bad, evil people," Mansfield said.

CHAPTER 12:
The 1993 Long Island Railway Shooting Rampage

Recently, many Western countries have been plagued with high profile mass shootings. Islamic extremists killed dozens of people in shooting attacks in Paris, France, in 2015 and 2016 and in the American cities of San Bernardino, California in 2015 and Orlando, Florida in 2016. There have also been some high profile shootings driven by racial and political animosity: a shooting of a predominately black church in Charleston, South Carolina, by a white supremacist and the recent shootings of multiple police officers in Dallas, Texas and Baton Rouge, Louisiana by black supremacists demonstrate that unfortunately sometimes people with axes to grind turn to violence for their solutions.

Before there were these most recent attacks, there was Colin Ferguson.

Colin Ferguson was a Jamaican immigrant who blamed others for his own inability to attain the American dream. Whites were the recipients of the majority of his vitriol, but Asians and blacks that he believed conspired with whites against him were also among his enemies. For years Ferguson ruminated about his pathetic existence and how he would one day exact his revenge against those who wronged him.

On December 7, 1993, Ferguson's rage boiled over when he took revenge on a Long Island rail car of innocent commuters, who wronged the man by merely existing because they happened to be white or Asian. When the smoke cleared, Ferguson's rampage of hate claimed six lives and left seventeen others wounded, some permanently.

Colin Ferguson's Early Life

Colin Ferguson was born on January 14, 1958, to a successful, affluent family in Jamaica. Growing up as a privileged Jamaican, Ferguson attended some of the best schools in the country and excelled in academics and sports such as cricket and soccer.

To anyone who knew Ferguson during his childhood, it seemed highly unlikely that the boy would grow up to become a notorious spree killer. He came from a stable family, received a good education, and showed no signs of violent tendencies towards animals or other children.

But as some of the other cases profiled in this book can attest to, there are usually problems underneath the façade of the public persona.

The young Ferguson was said to be spoiled and as he got older he came to expect a certain standard of living. Everything changed, though, when both his parents died in the late 1970s and he was left to fend for himself.

Broke and with no prospects in Jamaica, he came to the United States in 1982 on a tourist visa in order to game the system.

Most foreigners who enter the United States on a tourist visa are only allowed to stay for ninety days and are not permitted to work. If one overstays the visa, or finds work, then that person is subject to deportation.

Ferguson thought that the rules did not apply to him, so he overstayed his visa and looked for a full-time job. Since he did not have the proper work permits from the government, Ferguson was unable to find work other than menial labor.

Colin Ferguson was used to getting things his way in Jamaica, which in his mind meant that if things did not go his way in the United States forces must be at work against him. He began to blame the government, especially whites in the government, for his perceived problems. The fact that he simply did not follow the rules did not matter to the spree killer. He also took everything personally and began to believe that whites were conspiring against him personally.

But he knew that he could not keep the Immigration and Naturalization Service off his back forever and he also knew that if he were to get ahead in the United States, despite the racists he believed were out to get him, then he needed to get a green card.

To remedy the situation he did what thousands of others in his situation have done before and after: he married an American citizen!

Ferguson received permanent status to reside in the United States when he married Audrey Warren in 1986. It appears that the marriage was actually legitimate, at least to begin with, as the two stayed married until 1988. According to people who knew Ferguson during that time, the divorce from Warren shattered the Jamaican's already fragile ego. He became more withdrawn and although he still harbored an intense animosity towards whites, he began to focus his anger on women as well.

Somehow, despite his questionable resident status and his diminishing mental state, he found work as a security guard near his home on Long Island, New York. He was fired when he was injured on the job, which led to his first battle against the system in the form of a lawsuit from which he later won a settlement.

Instead of sitting around and waiting for his settlement, Ferguson enrolled in classes at Nassau Community College and actually showed some academic promise. He did well in all of his classes and made the Dean's List; but it was becoming increasingly difficult for Ferguson to hide his hatred and mental instability.

The Jamaican ex-pat began to argue with his professors and constantly injected race into class discussions, even when it was not remotely related to the topic at hand. His arguments with the professors became more heated and loud until he finally threatened violence on at least one occasion.

Threats of violence are taken extremely seriously on American college campuses, so Ferguson was expelled from Nassau Community College.

The Transition to a Race Warrior

A rational person would realize that threatening your professor will never turn out well.

But Colin Ferguson was not a rational person!

He let his hatred for whites stew while he sat alone in his apartment. He watched as whites drove down the street in new cars and he saw the nice new homes they lived in as took his daily ride on the train. Surely, Ferguson thought, the only reason why he did not have those things is because they were all out to get him.

Ferguson knew that his world view was correct and that if he were given the proper forum then others would agree, so after his expulsion from Nassau Community College, he transferred to the nearby Adelphi University in 1990.

After he transferred to Adelphi, Ferguson believed that he would meet others who were sympathetic to his increasingly extreme views. He began to speak openly in his classes of his contempt for whites and accused a female classmate of hurling racial epithets at him in the library.

The accusations proved to be false.

Ferguson then went to an anti-Apartheid symposium on the college campus, hoping to meet some fellow black radicals. Instead, he was angered to learn that the symposium allowed in whites and that the blacks conducting it were little more than "Uncle Toms" in Ferguson's twisted mind.

Alvin Makepela, a black African professor who helped sponsor the event, later told reporters about his run in with Ferguson during the symposium.

According to Makepela, Ferguson shouted from the audience and interrupted a scheduled speaker, saying, "We should be talking about the revolution in South Africa and how to get rid of the whites." The professor then exhorted Ferguson to let the speaker finish.

"You are one of those black people who have been employed at Adelphi to make sure black people don't succeed," was Ferguson's illogical response.

Ferguson continued with his racially tinged verbal tirades at Adelphi until the administration finally washed their hands of him with a suspension in June 1991.

For the next year and a half, Ferguson bounced from job to job, but he dedicated most of his time to the war he was to planning to bring to Long Island.

Colin Ferguson's Race War

Ferguson planned for his war by first legally buying a nine millimeter semi-automatic pistol and over 100 rounds of nine millimeter hollow point bullets. Hollow point bullets usually cause more destruction when they enter a human body because once they hit a bone they usually splinter into several pieces.

The shooter next had to find a target.

A mass shooting is one of the easiest terrorist attacks to plan and execute. The act can be done alone and it only requires a large crowd of people. In Ferguson's case the crowd needed to be white, but if some Asians and Hispanics were in the crowd that would be fine with him. Since he was living in Brooklyn right before he carried out his attack, Ferguson had access to plenty of targets in around Manhattan where plenty of white and Asian tourists would have been on hand.

But Ferguson's war was just as much a personal one as it was motivated by race and politics. Ferguson believed that his failures in life were caused by whites who were out to get him *personally*. Because of that, he decided to kill plenty of whites who wronged him in Long Island.

He decided that the daily commuter train that ran between the city and the Long Island suburbs would be the perfect location. It was crowded with plenty of whites, some of whom probably wronged him personally, and there was no place for them to run.

On December 7, 1993, Colin Ferguson bought an eastbound ticket to Long Island at the Brooklyn station near where he was living. After transferring trains at Penn Station, Ferguson boarded the third car of the eastbound train for Hicksville.

Just before the train reached the Merrilon Avenue Station, Ferguson began methodically walking towards the front of the car, shooting the white and Asian passengers in the process.

Almost immediately, the passengers realized what was happening and began to panic, causing a stampede that injured even more commuters.

Ferguson was able to empty two fifteen-round clips into twenty-five people in an approximately three minute span.

Finally, heroic passengers Mike O'Connor, Kevin Blum, and Mark McEntee wrestled Ferguson to the ground and took his weapon.

More passengers may have been saved, but once the situation became known to the Long Island Rail Road authorities, they ordered the doors to remain closed. Engineer Thomas Silhan ignored the order, climbed out of his cab, and then opened the doors of the car manually.

A Most Bizarre Trial

Once Colin Ferguson's massacre became public, a continuum of emotions were felt across the country from fear to anger. As elected officials tried to ease racial tensions in order to avoid reprisal attacks, it soon became clear to the Nassau County district attorney that Ferguson's murder trial would take on a circus-like atmosphere.

The case against Ferguson appeared open and shut: he killed his victims in front of plenty of witnesses and there were several anti-white statements he publically made that would go to prove motive.

But then famed leftist attorneys William Kunstler and Ron Kuby took the case.

Kunstler was noted for taking on many notable defendants, such as a prisoner in the 1971 Attica prison riot, during the 1960s and '70s. During the 1980s, he took Ron Kuby under his wing as his protégé and the duo became known for some rather eccentric defense techniques.

For Ferguson's defense, they argued that the Jamaican immigrant was driven insane from racism and that he was in fact the victim of "black rage."

The defense earned widespread dismissal by people across the United States who were following the case on the Court TV network. The defense was definitely unorthodox, but the reality was it was all they had.

And Ferguson was not willing to cooperate!

He fired Kunstler and Kuby and decided to represent himself during the trial.

The case proved to be one of the most entertaining and bizarre trials ever televised. Ferguson constantly referred to himself in third person, cross examined survivors with non-sequitur questions, and took the stand in his own defense.

While on the stand, Ferguson's explanations for the shooting went from the laughable to the truly bizarre. At first, he claimed that he was asleep during the shooting and that the true shooter planted the gun on him. He later claimed that a chip was implanted in his head by Asian scientists and that the Jewish Defense League was trying to kill him.

The jury wasted little time in deliberating and quickly came back with a guilty verdict on February 17, 1995. Ferguson was given a life sentence without the possibility of parole and was sent to the notoriously violent Attica state prison in upstate New York.

The Aftermath of the Shooting

Colin Ferguson's three minutes of carnage on the Long Island commuter train left deep scars across the country that have yet to heal and even behind bars Ferguson continues to feel the effects of his shooting spree.

Ferguson has not been one of the most popular inmates in the New York Department of Corrections. His beliefs and actions immediately put him at odds with the white inmates. While still awaiting trial in Nassau County, Ferguson was beaten by a group of white inmates and he has also experienced problems with inmates in Attica over the last two decades.

In one notable conflict, he fought with serial killer Joel Rifkin over use of a phone.

Ferguson told the serial killer, "I wiped out six devils, and you only killed women."

"Yeah, but I had more victims," Rifkin responded.

Ferguson then punched Rifkin, which earned him a stay in the segregation unit.

There is little doubt that we have not heard the last of Colin Ferguson, even from behind bars.

The shooting also became the cause for social debates in the American media. Instead of focusing on racial tensions, most of the news stories focused on gun control. The majority of opinion pieces took a pro-control stance and some argued for a ban on hollow point bullets.

The railway shooting was used by politicians to support the 1994 Assault Weapons Ban and helped launch the political career of Carolyn McCarthy.

McCarthy's husband Dennis was killed during the attack and her son Mike survived, but sustained permanent, debilitating injuries at the crazed shooter's hands. McCarthy won a seat in the U.S. House of Representatives that she held until she retired from Congress in 2015.

Politicians at the state level in New York followed the shooting by enacting some of the most restrictive gun laws in the United States, but not everyone was in favor of more gun laws.

A reaction to the initial calls for more gun control came through talk radio personalities of the 1990s, such as G. Gordon Liddy and Rush Limbaugh, who argued that more lenient gun laws may have actually saved lives. If New Yorkers were allowed to carry firearms the talk show hosts argued, then the shooter would have been stopped much sooner.

The reality is that Colin Ferguson was an extremely deranged man with a chip the size of Texas on his shoulder. If he had not killed the commuters on that train, he would have found another place and manner in which to kill people.

No law could have stopped Colin Ferguson.

Conclusion

The twelve cases profiled in this book prove that extreme acts of violence can happen anywhere, anytime, and to anyone. Developing countries and the United States do not have a monopoly on violence.

Some of these cases, such as the Mealin Road murder, were solved through advances in science, while others like the Maurin family murder were cracked by good old-fashioned police work and a mountain of circumstantial evidence.

Unfortunately, one of the most notorious crimes discussed here, the Keddie cabin murders, remains unsolved and probably will continue to be as the primary suspects are all deceased.

If there is one thing that you can get from all of these cases is to be prepared at all times. You might be on a commuter train after work or picking your children up from school and disaster can strike in the form of a deranged person.

Keep your head up and your eyes and ears open at all times!

GET ONE OF MY AUDIOBOOKS FOR FREE

audible
an amazon company

If you haven't joined Audible yet, you can get any of my audiobooks for FREE!
Go to www.JackRosewood.com to find out how!

More books by Jack Rosewood

Richmond, Virginia: On the morning of October 19, 1979, parolee James Briley stood before a judge and vowed to quit the criminal life. That same day, James met with brothers Linwood, Anthony, and 16-year-old neighbor Duncan Meekins. What they planned—and carried out—would make them American serial-killer legends, and reveal to police investigators a 7-month rampage of rape, robbery, and murder exceeding in brutality already documented cases of psychopaths, sociopaths, and sex criminals.

As reported in this book, the Briley gang were responsible for the killing of 11 people (among these, a 5-year-old boy and his pregnant mother), but possibly as many as 20. Unlike most criminals, however, the Briley gang's break-ins and robberies were purely incidental—mere excuses for rape and vicious thrill-kills. When authorities (aided by plea-bargaining Duncan Meekins) discovered the whole truth, even their tough skins crawled. Nothing in Virginian history approached the depravities, many of which were committed within miles of the Briley home, where single father James Sr. padlocked himself into his bedroom every night.

But this true crime story did not end with the arrests and murder convictions of the Briley gang. Linwood, younger brother James, and 6 other Mecklenburg death-row inmates, hatched an incredible plan of trickery and manipulation—and escaped from the "state-of-the-art" facility on May 31, 1984. The biggest death-row break-out in American history.

The world can be a very strange place in general and when you open the pages of this true crime anthology you will quickly learn that the criminal world specifically can be as bizarre as it is dangerous. In the following book, you will be captivated by mysterious missing person cases that defy all logic and a couple cases of murderous mistaken identity. Follow along as detectives conduct criminal investigations in order to solve cases that were once believed to be unsolvable. Every one of the crime cases chronicled in the pages of this book are as strange and disturbing as the next.

The twelve true crime stories in this book will keep you riveted as you turn the pages, but they will probably also leave you with more questions than answers. For instance, you will be left pondering how two brothers from the same family could disappear with no trace in similar circumstances over ten years apart. You will also wonder how two women with the same first and last names, but with no personal connections, could be murdered within the same week in the same city. The examination of a number of true crime murder cases that went cold, but were later solved through scientific advances, will also keep you intrigued and reading.

Open the pages of this book, if you dare, to read some of the most bizarre cases of disappearances, mistaken identity, and true murder. Some of the cases will disturb and anger you, but make no mistake, you will want to keep reading!

Of all the many psychopaths and sociopaths that have hunted for human victims throughout history, few have been more disturbing or mysterious than Christopher Bernard Wilder – the beauty queen killer. From the middle of the 1960s until 1984, Wilder sexually assaulted countless women and murdered at least nine in Australia and the United States. The beauty queen killer was not only a true psychopath, but also a hunter as he carefully chose attractive girls and young women to victimize. But Wilder was no creepy looking killer; he was an attractive, articulate man who used a camera and offers of a modelling career to get his unsuspecting, naïve victims to remote locations where he would then rape, torture, and ultimately kill them.

Among serial killer biographies, Wilder's is a cautionary tale. First as a juvenile and later as a young man, Wilder was arrested on numerous occasions for sexual assaults in both Australia and United States; but he never served any time behind bars due to technicalities, witnesses refusing to testify, or the judges showing sympathy towards the beauty queen killer. When one considers some of the better known American crime stories from history, many red-flags are apparent that point towards the future criminal potential of an individual: for Wilder, the flags were bright, crimson, quite large, and difficult to avoid, yet were ignored by his friends, family, and the authorities. Christopher Wilder's saga is therefore not just a true crime murder story, but also an unfortunate example of how the system can fail to protect the public from a known sexual sadist.

Open the pages of this intriguing book and read the story of an American serial killer who had it all: looks, money, and beautiful women. But as this captivating true crime story will reveal, nothing was ever enough for the beauty queen killer as he killed his way across the United States in order to satisfy his sadistic lust. Aspects of the Christopher Bernard Wilder story will disturb you, but at the same time you will find it difficult to put this serial killer biography down because you will be drawn in by the FBI's hunt to capture the elusive criminal.

GET THESE BOOKS FOR FREE

Go to www.jackrosewood.com

and get these E-Books for free!

A Note From The Author

Hello, this is Jack Rosewood. Thank you for reading this book. I hope you enjoyed the read. If you did, I'd appreciate if you would take a few moments to post a review on Amazon.

Here's the link to the book: Amazon

I would also love if you'd sign up to my newsletter to receive updates on new releases, promotions and a FREE copy of my Herbert Mullin E-Book, visit www.JackRosewood.com

Thanks again for reading this book, make sure to follow me on Facebook.

Best Regards

Jack Rosewood

Printed in Great Britain
by Amazon